A Thought to be Rehearsed
Aphorism in Wallace Stevens's Poetry

Studies in Modern Literature, No. 9

A. Walton Litz, General Series Editor

Consulting Editor for Titles on James Joyce
Professor of English
Princeton University

Other Titles in This Series

A Thought to be Rehearsed

Aphorism in Wallace Stevens's Poetry

by
Beverly Coyle

UMI RESEARCH PRESS
Ann Arbor, Michigan

The frontispiece photograph was taken by Rollie McKenna, known
for her portraits of British and American poets. Her photographs
illustrate *The Modern Poets,* edited by Malcolm Brinnin and Bill
Read, and *The Days of Dylan Thomas* by Bill Read.

Produced and distributed by
UMI Research Press
an imprint of
University Microfilms International
Ann Arbor, Michigan 48106

Library of Congress Cataloging in Publication Data

Coyle, Beverly.
   A thought to be rehearsed.

   (Studies in modern literature ; no. 9)
   A revision of thesis, University of Nebraska, 1974.
   Bibliography: p.
   Includes index.
   1. Stevens, Wallace, 1879-1955—Style. 2. Aphorisms
and apothegms. I. Title. II. Series.

PS3537.T4753Z623 1983   811'.52   83-5778
ISBN 0-8357-1414-4

To Mel Lyon

Contents

Acknowledgments

The dedication of this book expresses, however inadequately, my extensive debt to Melvin E. Lyon. While I am quick to own the flaws inherent in this study of subtle poetry, much of what may be useful here developed under his careful guidance and generous advice. He is a man completely devoted to literature and its students.

Many other expressions of thanks are in order here. I am especially grateful to A. Walton Litz for reading and commenting to immediate purpose on this text in its early stages, and for his continued support of my work over the years. I would also like to thank on behalf of so many Stevens scholars, Holly Stevens for her continued openness to questions she is asked to address from all quarters.

A small part of my work on this book was done during a year of study made possible by funds for faculty development from the Mellon Foundation, provided through Vassar College. I am grateful to many of my friends and colleagues at Vassar who have been enormously supportive of this project, and should like to mention particularly Susan Hawks Brisman, Kevin Cawley, Ann E. Imbrie, Michael Murray, and all the members of the Mellon Faculty Seminar.

I have had to call upon Sara S. Hodson many times for help in working with Stevens's manuscripts; her enthusiasm and expedition is representative of a general spirit of cooperation among the staff at the Huntington Library.

I wish to thank Rollie McKenna for her wonderful photograph of Stevens; the Huntington Library for permission to photograph the autograph material from Stevens's journal and *Adagia;* and Alfred A. Knopf, Inc., for permission to quote from the copyrighted editions of Stevens's poetry. The key to these editions will be as follows:

CP: *The Collected Poems of Wallace Stevens* (1954)
OP: *Opus Posthumous,* edited, with an introduction, by Samuel French Morse (1957)
 L: *Letters of Wallace Stevens,* edited by Holly Stevens (1966)

1

Preliminary Minutia

in the generations and becomings of our minds, anthologies,
good sayings are genes....

A.R. Ammons, *Sphere*[1]

This study examines "good sayings"—maxims, epigraphs and aphorisms—in Wallace Stevens's poems and provides an account of what they are doing there. Critics tend to acknowledge, dismiss, or otherwise comment on aphoristic expression as a stylistic issue, scolding Frost (for example) for his unfortunate sententiousness. But even in a time when "something there is that doesn't love a wall" is supposed to be more compelling than "Good fences make good neighbors," to some modern poets, good sayings are as compelling as anything else they consider poetic. This is particularly true of Stevens, who entitled his thirty-nine published aphorisms *Materia Poetica,* and insisted in one of them that "Poetry and materia poetica are interchangeable terms."[2]

Aphorism is a basic unit of expression in Stevens's poetry. That this is true is more generally *felt* than understood—certainly more noted than fully analyzed. Stevens wrote hundreds of isolated aphorisms on poetry, the imagination, the world, and God. He kept them in proper notebooks and only once, very early on, did he ever publish the thirty-nine as a group. It is one thing for a critic to note that fact and find it interesting in perhaps the same minor way Stevens found it interesting to engage in the activity. It is another, more serious, matter for the critic to pause at the aphorism *in* the Stevens poem where it both does and does not partake of the same activity. Or to put it another way: it is all well and good to acknowledge a poet's bent for collecting his private sayings in penciled notebooks; but to call him aphoristic somewhere else—in the poem itself—is perhaps to call him names.

The immediate purpose of this study is to show how aphorisms in Stevens's poetry figure in the development of his art. In the process, it is hoped that something substantial will be added to discoveries of the poetic continuity—the accumulative whole—of his work.[3] Such discoveries have been important answers to polemic treatises of Stevens which give intrinsic value to one or the other of his so-called poetic styles; suggestive, concrete, lyrical, sensuous, or chastened, abstract, philosophical, discursive. Good critical analysis may always need to address itself in part to the relationship between extremes, and as a result will be as varied as the poems themselves. At whatever extreme, however, a straightforward confrontation with Stevens's use of aphorisms in and out of poems will rescue the term "aphoristic" from its easy application as a pejorative. And while there will be nothing in later chapters of this book that will defuse the term "aphoristic" as it is specifically applied to other poets, this first chapter will offer a definition which will help locate and thereby understand aphorism wherever it occurs.

A few positive remarks on the aphoristic in Stevens precede this present study and to some extent prompt it. Though there are some who say "aphoristic" when they mean didactic and others who say "aphoristic" merely in a passing description of a line here and there, others have used the term purposefully in the analysis of Stevens's wide variety of styles and formats. But even in these instances there are differences in opinion as to what truly constitutes aphoristic expression.[4] These differences may be healthy ones, but in an effort to pinpoint the contention, one critic has said, "defining and locating aphorism is a delicate business."[5] One cannot help but hear in "a delicate business" the suggestion of touchy matters involving qualms of conscience. Indeed, without definition, the terms aphorism and aphoristic are loaded. Without the limits of definition we are sometimes left with those of connotation.

Toward a Definition

Indirectly, Frank Doggett points the way in his contention that all of Stevens's poetry, from *Harmonium* to *The Rock*,[6] is poetry of thought or idea. He notes that because of the expository nature of Stevens's poetry, criticism of his work tends toward summaries and lists of his ideas. But he contends that, while Stevens's ideas resemble familiar philosophical concepts, "they are not developed as arguments but are given unsupported, as though they existed in simple immediacy without need of dialectic."[7] A definition of aphorism seems imminent—particles *given unsupported,* existing in *simple immediacy.* When Doggett defines "idea" in the common sense of the word—"an abstract assertion that is formulated by means of a gist or summary"[8]—a working definition begins to show itself.

Dictionaries and literary handbooks consistently use as the basis of their definitions for aphorism the element of *content*—variously called the "truth" of aphorism, or its expression of a "principle," "opinion," or "accepted belief." What is proposed in the present study is a definition which will shift the focus of concern away from an emphasis upon content to an emphasis on the formulation. It is this author's contention that a reader responds to a statement as an aphorism essentially because its formal and thematic elements create in him a sense of closure, what Barbara Herrnstein Smith calls finality and stability.[9] In Doggett's definition of "idea" as "an abstract assertion that is formulated by means of a gist or summary," it is the phrase *formulated by means of* that is most crucial and has not been fully explored. Exactly what goes into the formulation of an aphorism that makes it act as gist or summary?

Anyone familiar with Smith's brilliant analysis will recognize the present author's debt to her findings on the questions of how poems close, since they also bear in important ways on how aphorisms *en*close all that they contain. The word "aphorism" is derived from the Greek word, *aphorizein,* to mark off boundaries (i.e., to enclose). The sense that a boundary has been set is an accurate metaphorical way of expressing the sense of finality and stability that a reader experiences from a statement formulated in a terse and usually pointed way. In part this sense of boundary *can* be established through the reader's response to the content of the statement—that is through his recognition of or familiarity with what the statement means. But his basic and initial response to the statement as an aphorism will be to a seeming completeness in the formulation of a statement—a seeming completeness which does not depend at all upon his perception of meaning. It is this structure which gives to an aphorism that charged and self-contained quality which resists translations of its ideas into other statement, and, when an aphorism occurs in a larger verbal context, makes it resist clarification or modification by that context.

It would be generally agreed that the statement, "It is raining," is not an aphorism. We do not respond to it as we do the statement, "When it rains it pours," which in part can be described as a statement that both symbolizes and sums up, in metaphorical terms, the generally accepted belief that hardships in life seem to happen all at once. Yet such a description does not explain why the statement is an aphorism. To explain that, it is necessary to recognize what is evoked not only by the paraphrastic equivalent of the statement but by its specific composition. An aphorism, then, is a brief statement, whether isolated or in a larger verbal context, whose formal and thematic elements together create in the reader a sense that what is expressed is both final and stable.

An Iliad is a penny pad: Formal Elements

Smith defines formal elements as "those which arise from the physical nature of words . . . such features as rhyme, alliteration, and syllabic meter."[10] In general, in regard to aphorisms, they might be called the various sound properties of language which give centripetal force to aphorisms—the force that tends to impel parts of a thing toward a center. An important psychological factor involved in the finality of isolated aphorism is the reader's awareness even before he reads that the expression has a very limited extent. Even in one of the longest aphorisms Stevens ever wrote, formal elements act to shorten it:

> To give a sense of the freshness or vividness of life is a valid purpose for poetry. A didactic purpose justifies itself in the mind of the teacher; a philosophical purpose justifies itself in the mind of the philosopher. It is not that one purpose is as justifiable as another but that some purposes are pure, others impure. Seek those purposes that are purely the purposes of the pure poet.[11]

Important to the reader's awareness of the physical limits of aphorism is the formal element of alliteration in the last sentence, which helps to give a strong sense of stability and finality to the whole statement. Alliteration may be similarly effective in creating the centripetal quality of aphorism even when it does not involve initial sounds or stressed syllables. Kenneth Burke points out, for example, that phonetic "cognates" such as /m-b-p/, /f-v/, /n-d-t/, /ch-j-g/ or /z-s-sh/ may figure in what he calls "concealed alliteration"[12]:

> Merit in poets is as boring as merit in people. (*OP,* 157)
> Each age is a pigeon-hole. (*OP,* 157)

Burke also mentions the possibility of "acrostic alliteration" where a sequence of consonants recurs in scrambled order as in the last two words of each line of "Nudity at the Capital":

> But nakedness, wollen massa, concerns an innermost atom.   /r-m-t-t-m/
> If that remains concealed, what does the bottom matter?[13]   /t-m-m-t-r/

In "Life is the reflection of literature" (*OP,* 159), perhaps the alliteration could be described as "radial," since apart from the repeated /l/ in all three nouns, the central word "reflection" brings together the /f/ and /er/ sounds of "life" and "literature" respectively.

What Smith terms a "summative effect"[14] of alliteration can be observed in "Poetry is a means of redemption" (*OP,* 160) in which the sequence /p-t-r-m-n-s/ in "*Poetry . . . means*" recurs in the final word "*redemption*" ("tion" correlates with "s"). Another striking example of this kind of alliteration occurs in the fifth of a series of aphorisms which Stevens called "New England Verses":

> Lean encyclopaedists, inscribe an Iliad.
> There's a weltanschauung of the penny pad. (*CP,* 104)

A brief paraphrase of this aphorism's cryptic meaning is essential here to show, ironically, how formal elements impose themselves so quickly upon such a paraphrase. The speaker in line one asks of the unimaginative encyclopaedists (who ordinarily accumulate enormous volumes of information) that they merely copy down the Iliad. By doing so (line two) an entire world view can be contained in a very small space. The final phrases of the two lines bring together through rhyme the idea that all-encompassing perspectives such as the one in Homer's epic can be recorded on a small tablet; we also get in those phrases a new aphorism: "An Iliad is the penny pad." Vital to our sense of the aphoristic here is the repetition in "penny pad" of the /en-p-d/ sequence of "*encyclopaedists*". This is summative alliteration inseparable from idea: Vast A to Z compilations of facts confronting the *encyclopaedists* can be condensed in half the space (in *penny pads*).

Although a fuller discussion of syntax is more properly placed in the next section on thematic elements of aphorism, certain syntactic structures do set up sound repetitions that operate like formal elements. Numerous examples similar to the following one from *Adagia* can be cited throughout Stevens's poetry:

> Literature is the better part of life. To this it seems inevitably necessary to add, provided life is the better part of literature. (*OP*, 153)

Here formal repetition creates a series of mutually reinforcing echoes: "Literature is . . . life is," "the better part . . . the better part," "Literature . . . life . . . . life . . . literature." When Stevens says that "To be at the end of fact is not to be at the beginning of imagination but it is to be at the end of both," the formal "to be at" repetition is similarly reinforcing as it operates in conjunction with the strong thematic sequence ("end . . . beginning . . . end").

In addition to alliteration, formal devices of rhyme, meter, scansion, and pacing are important in analyzing the centripetal force of aphorism. The interrelationship of these devices is shown in the four-line aphorism by Stevens entitled "Adult Epigram":

> The romance of the precise is not the elision
> Of the tired romance of imprecision.
> It is the ever-never-changing same,
> An appearance of Again, the diva-dame. (*CP*, 353)

Again, a paraphrase for the sake of what cannot be paraphrased: the quatrain presents, in two sentences, two definitions of the "romance of the precise," Stevens's phrase for poetry which captures reality. The first definition is negative and abstract: poetry does not become a precise imaginative expression of reality merely by eliminating imaginative expression that fails of precision ("tired" seems to suggest imaginative expression that may once have been precise but has ceased to be so as reality and man's sense of it have changed).

The second definition is positive and more concrete because of its use of personification: the poetry of reality is an imaginative expression (or "appearance," in the sense of "appearance and reality") of the constantly and subtly evanescent stability ("same") of existence—an image of reality, not as a solid "is" but as a moment-to-moment recurrence with faint modifications ("Again"). Stevens is addressing himself to the poet's problem of bridging the gulf between ultimate reality and its various appearances. The difficulty of giving this problem exact expression is captured in the two daring phrases of lines 3 and 4—"the ever-never-changing same," "An appearance of Again, the diva-dame"—the first one abstractly expressing the evasive and paradoxical relationship of permanence and flux, the second personifying that paradox as reality itself.

But such a paraphrase has very little to do with the aphoristic qualities of this quatrain. In reading it we have a sense of completeness, a sense that what is said is all that can or need be said, despite any confusion on our part about its meaning and consequent desire to have it explained. What we initially recognize and respond to is the aphoristic finality and stability that we experience when we come to the end of the quatrain. There is a tension between this experience of completeness and the uncertainty we may feel about the meaning: that is, though we may not know exactly what the meaning is, we feel that it is somehow fully contained within the strict boundaries of the short statement. One obvious formal element which produces cohesive or centripetal force in the four lines is the occurrence of rhyme (aabb). This alone, however, is not enough to stabilize the statement.[15] Rhyme can, in fact, have the opposite effect: it may increase the reader's expectation of more rhyme (in this case, cc dd ee ff, etc.). But there is a significant relationship between rhyme and the movement of the aphorism toward its final-sounding end. The opening couplet ends in a feminine rhyme while the rhyme of the last couplet falls on strongly stressed syllables. Such a shift from weaker to a stronger rhyme corresponds to the movement of the idea in the aphorism from negative to positive assertion. Further reinforcing this movement is the variation of rhythmic feet from line to line:

The rōmánce ōf thē precíse īs nót thē elísīon
Ōf the tíred rōmánce ōf ímprecísion.
Īt iś thē évēr-névēr-cĥanging sáme,
Āñ áppéaráñce óf Āgáin, the dívā-dáme.

Because there is a reduction in the number of unstressed syllables after line one, the strong four beats of the lines which follow contribute to a sense of closure. The use of iambic feet in the last three lines also contributes to this movement, especially the concentration of this shorter foot in "thē évēr-névēr-cĥangīng sáme" and "Āgáin, thē divā-dáme." Stevens further sets off these two key phrases of his definition by interjecting end-line and mid-line pauses, in contrast to the absence of pauses in lines 1 and 2. Still other formal devices operate in these key phrases, both to set them off from lines of 1 and 2 and to pull them together and thereby stabilize lines 3 and 4. Long vowel /ā/ and nasal /m/ and /n/ sounds dominate both phrases; the consonantal /v/ and /g/ sounds of the first phrase are repeated in the /v/, /g/ (and g's related /ch/) sounds of the second phrase; the harsh /r/ sounds emphasized by hyphenation and internal rhythm in "ever-never-changing same" gives way to the harsh /d/ sounds emphasized by hyphenation and caesura in "Again, the *d*iva-*d*ame."

When I turn to the occurrence of these formal elements of aphorism within a poetic context, I shall show how their use is of particular significance in setting off the aphorism from the rest of the poem. Particular boundary effects can be achieved, for example, when the aphorism employs devices not used throughout the poem, thus drawing attention and giving centripetal force to a portion or portions of the poem: rhyme or the termination of rhyme; employment or abandonment of rhythmic devices; a shift from or toward monosyllabic diction; an assonantal or consonantal dominance in the aphoristic portion of the poem.[16]

Life is composed of propositions about it: Thematic Elements

Thematic elements are defined as "those which arise from the symbolic or conventional nature of words and to which only someone familiar with the language could respond"—features which "include everything from syntax to tone."[17] Some thematic elements have already been dealt with indirectly in my earlier analysis of the interrelationship of thematic movement and formal elements. This section, however, will discuss thematic elements which characterize a particular type of aphorism whose finality and stability establish an authoritative posture which is ultimate sounding, assertive, or definitive.

Dominating the *Adagia* and Wallace Stevens's later poetry is the occurrence of aphorisms whose centripetal force is produced not primarily by their formal elements but by their use of simple (or predicative) sentence structure and by the apparent absence of modifiers, qualifying phrases, and subordinate clauses. Frank Doggett has noted that a common type of sentence in the later poetry uses a subject and some form of the verb "to be," followed by a predicate nominative or a predicate adjective phrase:

Imagination is the will of things. (*CP*, 84)

Man's soil is his intelligence. (*CP*, 28)

Sentimentality is a failure of feeling. (*OP*, 162)

The mind is the terriblest force in the world. (*CP*, 436)

Doggett contends that the "relationships and conjunctions of concepts" which appear in such predicative sentences are effects that resemble those of metaphor. Here, he asserts, the predicate nominative "says that one image, one concept, one substantive, is equal to another, although by the very statement of equivalence ... it is implied that the equality is really an identity of aspects and a separation of essences, like the relationships in metaphor." However, when he goes on to call the predicate nominative construction the "sentence of definition," he notes that it is distinguished from metaphor by its dogmatic, aphoristic tone. He concludes that the frequent occurrence of this type of sentence "gives the effect of axiom, its accepted verity and essential rightness."[18]

Josephine Miles, in her book, *Style and Proportion,*[19] gives support to these brief comments regarding the relationship between sentence structure and aphoristic style. She says that there are essentially three traditional styles in English, each based upon variations and combinations of one of three basic sentence-types: the "adjectival style," based on the "adjectival sentence"; the "classical style," based on the "connective-subordinative sentence"; and the "aphoristic style," based upon the "predicative sentence." She distinguishes between the three sentence-types and their respective styles by calculating the ratio of grammatical elements occurring in representative passages of prose or poetry. The crucial point for the purpose of the current study is Miles's contention that the use of predicative sentences accounts for the way thoughts "seem to repel rather than attract one another." By the word "repel" she suggests how the thematic device of sentence structure creates in the reader a sense that individual sentences (and individual statements of idea) are *self-contained*—that they are what Doggett refers to as statements which are dogmatic and axiomatic, and what have been referred to as "centripetal" statements in the present analysis. A lack of connectives between thoughts tends to heighten the authoritative tone of individual statements, giving to each statement an independence apart from the larger verbal context.[20]

Similarly the lack of qualifying words (adjectives or other qualifying phrases) can give to predicative sentences a convincing, authoritative tone. Barbara Smith discusses this phenomenon by considering the following series of assertions: *He probably tells the truth; No doubt he tells the truth; I do believe he tells the truth; I assure you he tells the truth; He tells the truth.* She contends that the last assertion is "the most convincing" and hence the most aphoristic:

for even where the qualifying phrases have been added [in the first four sentences] to strengthen credibility, they actually have the effect of weakening it. They suggest that the speaker has some reason to emphasize the validity of his assertion, and our experience with our own speech and that of others will make us sense that among those reasons is his own doubt of its validity or his recognition of the grounds for his listener's doubt.[21]

1. Autograph entries from *Adagia*.

Happiness is an acquisition

Progress in any aspect is a movement through changes of terminology

The highest pursuit is the pursuit of happiness on earth.

L'art d'être heureux

Goethe's General-Beichte was written of another who "spake three thousand proverbs, and his songs were a thousand and five. From Goethe proverbs poured incessantly."

                Goethe : Fairley ⊙ Univ P, 1932.

Each age is a pigeon-hole.

The stream of consciousness is individual; the stream of life is total. Or, the stream of consciousness is individual; the stream of life, total.

To give a sense of the freshness or vividness of life is a valid purpose for poetry. A didactic purpose justifies itself in the mind of the teacher; a philosophical purpose justifies itself in the mind of the philosopher.

The last assertion, however, which Smith calls the *unqualified assertion,* "conveys a sense of the speaker's security, conviction, and authority. Since he did not guard or cover himself with implicit or explicit reservations, we assume that he did not need to."[22]

Smith also notes that there exists a whole set of words and phrases which produce effects similar to that of such unqualified assertion. Consider the italicized words of the following aphorisms by Stevens:

The *ultimate* value is reality. (*OP,* 73)

Reality is the spirit's *true* center. (*OP,* 85)

Imagination is the *only* genius. (*OP,* 108)

It is necessary to propose an enigma to the mind. The mind *always* proposes a solution. (*OP,* 108)

The universals "ultimate" and "true," the absolutes "only" and "always" are, Smith says, "qualifiers grammatically" but are "nonqualifying in expressive function."[23] She also notes that a similar effect—that is, an effect of conviction and authority—can be produced by the superlative form of the adjective,

Reality is the object seen in its *greatest* common sense. (*OP,* 101)

by all-embracing nouns,

Everything tends to become real; or *everything* moves in the direction of reality. (*OP,* 43)

and by the insisting subjunctive,

Poetry *must* be irrational. (*OP,* 28)

While I do not want to imply that all predicative sentences, unqualified assertions, or sentences which utilize unqualifying words or phrases are aphorism, it is important to see that such thematic elements of sentence structure and word choice can produce a tone which is aphoristic in that it contributes to a reader's sense that what has been said is all that need or can be said. W.H. Auden puts it this way: "The aphorist does not argue or explain, he asserts; and implicit in his assertion is a conviction that he is wiser or more intelligent than his readers."[24]

An apple serves as well as any skull: Predeterminative Effects

An anecdote will most quickly illustrate Smith's analysis of the interplay between formal and thematic elements in a sequence which sets up and confirms the reader's expectation. A certain composer's valet is said to have gotten his master out of bed in the mornings by playing the first seven notes of a favorite harmonic scale. According to the story the composer then felt compelled to get dressed hurriedly and rush to the piano in order to play the final note for himself. The scale corresponds roughly to what Smith calls a thematic element, the eighth note in that scale to a formal element. The composer's recognition of the sequence of seven notes and his desire to hear the eighth one corresponds to the setup and confirmation of expectation which is the basis of predetermination.[25]

Predetermination in Stevens's aphorisms is employed with great subtlety and its effect is largely comic:

If the answer was frivolous, the question was frivolous (*OP,* 175)

Just as there is always a romantic that is potent, so there is always a romantic that is impotent. (*OP,* 180)

Literature is not based on life but on propositions about life, of which this is one. (*OP,* 171)

In each of these examples centripetal force is produced not only by the formal reinforcement of alliteration, assonance, and repetition of whole word sounds but by thematic reinforcement as well—by syntatic structures which have strongly predetermined or expected counterparts. In the phrase, "If the answer was frivolous," the "if" sets up the reader for the implied "then" phrase. Moreover, the pairing of "question" after "then" with "answer" after "if," plus the repetition of "frivolous," further contribute to the reader's sense that the aphorism is complete or final by increasing his feeling of an expectation that has been confirmed. Similar syntactic structures appear in "Just as... so," "not... but," and again they work together with formal elements to set up and confirm the reader's expectation. Predeterminative effects can occur in the careful placement of cognates:

Literature is the *abnormal* creating an illusion of the *normal.* (*OP,* 177)

The balancing of antithetical words is also strongly "confirming" to the reader:

To live *in* the world but *outside* of existing conceptions of it. (*OP,* 164)

Sometimes parallelism and antithesis are set up in almost mathematical proportions:

> The eye sees less than the tongue says. The tongue says less than the mind thinks. (*OP*, 170)

> Poetry has to be something more than a conception of the mind. It has to be a revelation of nature. Conceptions are artificial. Perceptions are essential. (*OP*, 164)

In another type of predetermination, stability and finality tend to be achieved not when the reader's expectations are confirmed but rather, when they are denied. In this case the interplay of formal and thematic elements also works toward a stable conclusion, but it is one which opposes that anticipated by the reader. The strong cohesive form of this type of aphorism is prevalent in the aphorisms found in the *Harmonium* poems.

The interplay of sound and syntactic elements in the following four-line aphorism from "Le Monocle de Mon Oncle" is representative of the success Stevens would finally achieve in integrating aphorisms into the total poem. It serves as what he will term "an anchorage of thought," yet is carefully embedded in the narrator's lyrically expressed feelings about transience and death:

> An apple serves as well as any skull
> To be the book in which to read a round,
> And is as excellent, in that it is composed
> Of what, like skulls, comes rotting back to ground.
> (*CP*, 14)

The aphorism has two parts—a setup (in the first three and one half lines) in which the reader's expectations are dictated by certain predetermining devices and a surprise conclusion withheld until after the second caesura of the last line. Both parts work toward a stable conclusion, but a conclusion that opposes the one anticipated by the reader. The major clue as to the end of the aphorism is implicitly presented in the comparison between the apple, a synecdoche for physical love and youth, and the skull, the "fruit" or final product of death and the symbol for where life's passions end. But countering this grim theme is the setup's subtle allusion to Eden—that earthly paradise—and especially its implication (with or without the allusion) that the apple is an even better symbol for human destiny than the skull because of its connotation of natural life, pleasure, and sensuality. In the setup, the play on the key words "round," "excellent" and "composed" contribute strongly to connotations of natural pleasure and sensuality. Also, the length of the word "excellent," the placing of the caesura immediately after it, and the slight delay of the conclusion which the caesura causes, all help to put emphasis upon "excellent" as the summing-up of the tone of the setup. At this point, with the reader's expectation of a continuation of that tone also at a climax, the aphorism proceeds, after a neutral series of words ("in that it is composed/Of what"), to undercut that tone completely and reverse its connotations in the final phrase, "comes rotting back to ground." The reader's expectations are wittily defeated as he receives a shock of surprise *and* recognition: the relationship between apple and skull is suddenly, ironically, and fully understood in terms which were suggested but deliberately played down in the setup. The apple is now viewed as an "excellent" death image—an image of death-in-life—because the process of its life cycle (and especially its conclusion) represents the similar cycle (and especially the conclusion) of a human being's life, particularly of his passion and sexuality. Other words in the setup also take on new meaning as a result of this shift in perspective. Both apple and skull are "composed" of what inevitably decomposes, and "round" carries the connotation of the cyclical transience of life and sensuality. Also, the use of "skulls," "rotting," and the terminal word "ground" adds to the centripetal force of the aphorism.

On the Road Home

And now it is possible to deepen our working definition by suggesting something of the phenomenological implication inherent in the way aphorisms function. A phenomenological account may clear up the issue with which we began—why it is that defining aphorism is a *delicate business;* and why Litz, for example, in describing the aphorisms in "The Man with the Blue Guitar," emphasizes not their centripetality, but something apparently opposite: the way they "seem to demand expansion or interpretation"[26] which might suggest a lack of stability or finality.

The centripetal, inward force of aphorism is the one suggested by those pointing hands appearing in the margins of early scholastic and, later, Renaissance texts. William Painter's edition of Chaucer, for example, has printed hands in the margins so that readers uninterested in the stories might easily locate the moral. The hands say in effect, "Look. Here is the general truth of this matter, the law, the rule of conduct it offers to be taken to heart by you. This is the message, the given." An aphorism's easy citation is part of its quality as a given. One might call this the scholastic program for aphorism. The pointing hand signals the *deductive* stance—reasoning from the general: "Art is long, life is short."

But the opposite centrifugal force in aphorism is the one most fully defined by Francis Bacon in an effort to suppress the scholastic program. Bacon defined aphorism as a detached item of empirical fact drawn from direct observation. He was not arbitrarily changing the scholastic sense of the word. Bacon found authority for his change. In fact, he turned to Hippocrates for his model where the most typical aphorism is not a general truth at all, but a detail so factual that it is medical. Bacon describes Hippocrates as a man "much given to experiments and observation, not striving after words or methods, but picking out the very nerves of science and so setting them forth."[27] The desystematizing of knowledge, and the presentation of it in detached aphorisms becomes the basis of Bacon's inductive reasoning; aphorisms are a means by which new knowledge grows out of old because "this delivering of knowledge in distinct and disjointed aphorism doth leave the wit of man more free to turn and to toss, and to make use of that which is delivered to more several purposes and application."[28]

Now something of the pointing hand image still applies to Bacon's notion of aphorism, but one would have to draw the hand in a different way rather than in the margin, where it seems to ask one to note closely and then accept what is said as a *given.* To represent a Baconian aphorism, one would want to draw the hand *around* the particle of information one is calling an aphorism because it is less a given than a projective; not the message itself, but the message bearer. So, we have two opposite forces for aphorism: something that *is* and something that is *doing.* One might recall those worried messengers who show up in the royal courts. Typically they beg the king's pardon and hope the messenger will not be associated with the message. They suffer terribly in their predicament. Allow that predicament to stand for something of this phenomenological account defining the tension we feel in aphorisms. When they occur, are they general truths one can point to with a pointing hand? Or are they rather specific observations pointing beyond themselves? Apparently they cannot be both at once, at least not easily.

Pointing hands have been placed in the margins of the Stevens poem, "On the Road Home," and then crossed out in order to suggest this play between the scholastic aphorism and the Baconian aphorism—the centripetal and centrifugal forces:

It was when I said,
"There is no such thing as the truth,"
That the grapes seemed fatter.
The fox ran out of his hole.

You... You said,
"There are many truths,
But they are not parts of a truth."
Then the tree, at night, began to change,

Smoking through green and smoking blue.
We were two figures in a wood.
We said we stood alone.

It was when I said,
☜ *"Words are not forms of a single word.*
In the sum of the parts, there are only the parts.
The world must be measured by eye."

It was when you said,
☜ *"The idols have seen lots of poverty,*
Snakes and gold and lice,
But not the truth."

It was at that time, that the silence was largest
And longest, the night was roundest,
The fragrance of the autumn warmest,
Closest and strongest. (*CP,* 201)

Often a Stevens poem will invite a reader to accept its aphorisms as givens. This requires cooperation; and we cooperate most readily when the aphorisms, like those in "On the Road Home," concur with what we ourselves already believe or think to be at the heart of Stevens's belief, or at the heart of a shared Weltanschauung. Any number of modernists, including Stevens, may have said, "There's no such thing as the truth," or may have said, as a wry version of the same thing, "In the sum of the parts, there are only the parts." Taking the aphorisms in this poem as givens has led to such traditional interpretations of "On the Road Home" as the one Sukenick offers: "One may... enjoy a pleasurable relation with reality in which the ego demands from the chaos of reality nothing but what it can give, and chaos is therefore adequate to satisfy the desires of the ego."[29] Indeed, the given, "There is no such thing as the truth," repeated in various ways in the poem, seems to be what is taken to heart by the speakers in the poem: when we felt the truth of no truth at all that night on the road home, we began to measure the world as we should—through the senses; sensual beauty came forward and was largest, longest, closest, and strongest; that is all the "truth" there is.

However, this is not the only way the aphorisms work. Below is a passage from Stevens's journal which is his witty account of the phenomenological play between aphorism as given (the scholastic program) and aphorism as projective (the Baconian program):

There are no end of gnomes that might influence people—but do not. When you first feel the truth of, say, an epigram, you feel like making it a rule of conduct. But this one is displaced by that, and things go on in their accustomed way. There is one pleasure in this volitile morality: the day you believe in chastity, poverty and obedience, you are charmed to discover what a monk you have always been—the monk is suddenly revealed like a spirit in a wood; the day you turn Ibsenist, you confess that, after all, you always were an Ibsenist, without knowing it. So you come to believe in yourself, and in your new creed.[30]

Both the given and the projective programs behind the use of aphorism are suggested here. First, Stevens says that when we initially feel the truth of an epigram we feel like making it a rule of conduct (the scholastic program). "On the Road Home" is in part about this first stage—not only the inevitability but the importance of seizing on a saying as the truth, letting it change our lives and the world; grapes become sweeter, trees start to smoke, the night's fragrance becomes warmer, closer, stronger than it has ever been. When we take the truth to heart, expecting our love to last forever, we are yielding to what the scholastic pointing finger insists: "Here," it says, "take note, take heart, act accordingly." The speakers in the poem are charmed by what is suddenly "revealed like a spirit in a wood." In their enthusiasm, they repeat what they always knew: *I said, then you said, then I said. Yes, we were sure that was it.*

But just as in this journal entry we have a Stevens reflecting, thinking back, on what this experience means in terms of a pattern of experiences with these truths over time, so too in the poem there is a present speaker who is remembering this "on the road home" experience in the past and considering the implication of that distance between the past and the present. Things have gone on in the meantime. Aphorisms are replaced by others; first the monk, then the Ibsenist, then the atheist in us is revealed. Only in this way, through these pieces of experience, do we come into our belief, our creed, our selves built up over time. The speaker in the present does not say, in present tense, "It was when we *say* (once and for all) there's no such thing as the truth," that we feel the truth of that forever. Rather, he is remembering how it *was* when he seized on these givens. The incident as having passed is repeated like a refrain in four out of six stanzas: "It was *when* I said ... It was when .... It was when .... It was at *that* time." The distance between the then and the now in both the poem and the journal entry is essential to what Stevens has observed about a gnome's double program. First it is seized and believed in such a way that we feel the impulse to fix it with that pointing hand as an unassailable truth. But in time its message becomes subordinate to other messages which it projects, just as Hippocrates's aphorisms, as Bacon understood them, build bit by bit toward conclusions which in turn are subservient to larger conclusions. Only a naive disposition toward agnosticism that we possess ourselves, or assume Stevens possessed, makes us inclined, ironically, to respond to these negative sayings as fixed in Stevens. Did Stevens ever say, "There's no such thing as the truth"? Throughout his criticism one finds it seized as a given by critics who would otherwise never think of themselves as didactic.[31] The journal entry and the poem, however, demonstrate that this could never be an ultimate truth. The poem as a whole had become one bit, one moment when one of those truths became intense and radiantly apparent in a series of such moments. If we have faith enough to seize the given when it presents itself, and, paradoxically, if we have patience enough to observe the givens within a Baconian series pointing elsewhere, then we will find our way home: "So you come to believe in yourself and in your new creed."

This account of the given/projective paradox may alert us to the fact that in our own naive disposition we may be inclined to take as given only those sayings most consonant with our own. We point to them with the modern equivalent of a pointing hand—pencil underlinings, marginal checks— reminders that we should pause here and take note when what a poet says seems closest to our own skepticism, to "no ideas but in things" so often reduced to "no ideas at all."

Ammons, in his poem entitled "Essay on Poetics," suggests how we might get ourselves out of the impasse through a program of not fewer but *more* aphorisms:

>   ... "no ideas but
>
> in things" can be read into alternatives—"no things but in ideas,"
> "no ideas but in ideas," and "no things but in things"; one thing
> always to keep in mind is that there are a number of possibilities[32]

And to return for a moment to Ammons's metaphor—"good sayings are genes"—and to remember all the possibilities, it is perhaps pertinent to note that some radical geneticists may shock us by regarding human beings as merely devices to guarantee the survival of *genes,* even as thinkers like Stevens may prefer to regard poems as devices useful for the survival of *aphorisms.*

2

An Anchorage of Thought

Stevens indicated very early a liking for the way words are used in aphorisms. In the journal he kept between 1898 and 1912, he repeatedly records his delight in the aptness of words so used, their precision, and hence the sense of truth one has on reading them. In 1910, he wrote to Elsie Moll, his future wife, that among his "jottings of things to think about" he liked to keep lists of "epigrams." He gave the following example: "The greatest pleasure is to do a good action by stealth, and have it found out by accident," to which he added, "(could any true thing be more amusing?)." Something akin to such apt expression seems to have been his own aim when he wrote in his journal. There, in a very early entry, he notes that "it is a great pleasure to seize an impression and lock it up in words: you feel as if you had it safe forever" (*L*, 30). He was also studying writers who wrote aphorisms. Running throughout the journal are such comments as the following:

> Have just finished Leopardi's "Pensieri".... They are paragraphs on human nature, like Schopenhauer's psychological observations, Paschals *(sic)* "Pensées, Rochefoucauld's "Maximes" etc. How true they all are! I should like to have a library of such things. (*L*, 88)

Stevens eventually came to own many volumes of collected aphorisms[1] and some of his later journals consisted almost exclusively of his own aphorisms and of aphoristic passages copied from books and reviews. Similarly, it was also an early habit of his to jot down at random short statements about a variety of subjects which he either found in his reading or invented himself. Frequently, he would record short passages written by others and then respond to them with short *pensées* of his own:

> Read in Matthew Arnold's "Notebooks" this morning: "la destination de l'homme est d'accroître le sentiment de la joie, de féconder l'énergie expansive, et de combattre, dans tout ce qui sent, le principe de l'avilissement et les douleurs."
>
> As far as one thing by itself can be true, that is true, I think; but for the word "destination" I should substitute "virtue." Yet it is only one phase of "infinite" wisdom, like the fear of the Lord etc. (*L*, 87-88)[2]

2. Autograph from journal: the entry in which Stevens says he'd
    like to have a library of aphorisms.

He included many quotations in his letters to Elsie and although he sometimes apologized for doing so ("quotations are fatal to letters," he once wrote her), his enjoyment for "such things" tended to override his misgivings. After his death, Mrs. Stevens preserved parts of his letters for scholars and much of what she selected are aphorisms:

> The only brilliant things in life are friendship, self-denial, and similar evidences of civilization, as far as men are concerned.

> The young man with his star, or the young woman with her dreams are not as happy as the man with his cow—and the woman with her knitting.

> Life is a very, very thin affair except for the feelings; and the feelings of home waters the richest garden of all—the freshest and sweetest.

> Homer's only a little story—and so are all the others: and yet men have not memory enough even to remember a little story. It is a tremendous mark of scholarship to know a little story.[3]

The contents of Stevens's notes during these years cover a wide range of interests and concerns about poetic expression. A comment Stevens would later make about one of his *Harmonium* poems provides a helpful interpretation of the concerns of some of the notes. Stevens said, "I'm sorry that poems of this kind have to contain any ideas at all because their sole purpose is to fill the mind with images and sounds that they contain" (*L,* 251). Many of the entries are comprised of brief, self-contained images and sounds:

> The peaks to the South shelve off into the heavens. Snow & cloud become confused. And the blue distances merge mountain and sky into one (*L,* 66)

> At gomorrah, I forgot the whirring of the locust. The sound is everywhere in the trees today. It starts low & then rises until just before it stops. And it sounds, perfectly, like a field-noise at harvest (*L,* 78)

The largest part of the journal entries, however, reveal Stevens's intense interest in poetry for the ideas or thought it contains. He records in 1906:

> Been reading poetry. What strikes me is the capable, the marvellous, poetic language; and the absence of poetic thought. Modern people have never failed to crown the poet that gave them poetic thought .... We get plenty of moods (and like them, wherever we get them ...); and so we get figures of speech, and superb lines, and fantastic music. But it's the mind we want to fill—with Life. We admit now that Truth is the warrior and Beauty only his tender hide, as one might say. (*L,* 92)

It is difficult to state exactly what Stevens means by "poetic thought" in this entry. He separates "poetic thought" from "poetic language" ("figures of speech," "impressions," "superb lines," "fantastic music") and apparently the meaning of "poetic thought" is bound up in his insistence that ultimately the role of poetry is "to fill the mind—with Life"—which has to do with expressing the truth or idea of experience as well as its beauty. He notes in another entry that the "mind cannot always live in a 'diviner either.' The lark cannot always sing at heaven's gate. There must exist *a place to spring from*—a refuge from the heights, *an anchorage of thought*" (*L,* 27). During this time Stevens began to view a connection between such poetic thought and its expression in aphorism as able to provide him with such a "refuge" or "place to spring from." For example, after quoting for Elsie a passage from the literary critic Paul Elmer More, Stevens writes:

> My mind is rather full of such things to-day, and so resembles the mood that fastened me, a year or more ago, on Matthew Arnold—and maxims! ... To think occasionally of such

things gives me a comforting sense of balance and makes me feel like the Brahmin on his mountain-slope who in the midst of his contemplation—surveyed distant cities—and then plunged in thought again. (*L,* 133)

3.   Autograph from journal.

Once as I looked up I saw a big, pure drop of rain slip from one leaf to another of a clematis vine. The thought occurred to me that it was just such quick, unexpected, commonplace, specific things that poets and other observers jot down in their note-books. It was certainly a most keen pleasure to be able to be specific about such a thing.

His concern for the way the mind fluctuates between heights and depths of feeling and thought, his interest in tracing these movements, and his belief in the place of aphoristic expression in finding a "balance" between them—these are the important developments for Stevens during this time when he wrote very little poetry. As we shall see, aphorisms *in* poems are a measure of Stevens's love for "the feel of truth [in] an epigram" despite his belief that "one is displaced by that, and things go on in their accustomed way" (*L,* 91). They are also an indication of his belief in the understanding that aphorism gives the mind and in the resulting self-discovery which he would later describe as the momentary balance between reality and the imagination. Finally, aphorisms in

4. Autograph from journal: "There must be a place to spring from... *an anchorage of thought.*"

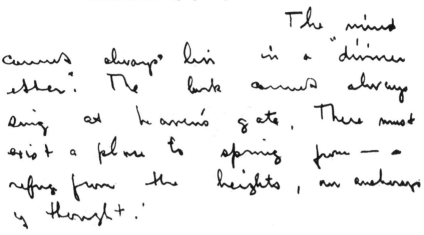

poems reflect Stevens's theory that the aphoristic expression of that balance intensifies experience by helping us discover, amidst the multiplicity of our potential selves, a self that is momentarily stable in a world of constant change. Thus the function of aphorism in poetry is not to capture permanently or didactically some absolute truth, but to give imaginative man a momentary hold on an aspect of experience through the power of his own expression.

Nowhere is this purpose more clearly demonstrated than in the *Adagia,* a formal collection of original aphorisms begun in 1930, fifteen years after the note-taking period. A brief description of the *Adagia* at this point will illuminate the discussion of the early notes in which Stevens's interest in aphorism began and of his early poems, whose structures reflect that interest.[4]

For every point in the *Adagia* there is counterpoint. Its whole method is one of balancing propositions against each other. Some of the aphorisms address themselves directly to the activity of "balancing". Scattered throughout the journal, they suggest to the reader the speaker's attitude about writing aphorisms:

Life is a composite of propositions about it. (*OP,* 171)

Literature is based not on life but on propositions about life, of which this is one. (*OP,* 171)

It is necessary to propose an enigma to the mind. The mind always proposes a solution. (*OP,* 168)

Thought tends to collect in pools. (*OP,* 170)

Stevens skillfully employs formal and thematic elements to give these aphorisms that pleasing sense of truth he enjoyed in the aphorisms of Arnold, Pascal, and others. But he also employs another technique that tends to play across the boundarylike authority of individual entries. This is the technique of counterpoint—the tendency for one proposition to stand in contrapuntal relationship to another. Below, for example, is a grouping of six *adagia* on "thought":

1. There is nothing in life except what one thinks of it.
2. Accuracy of observation is the equivalent of accuracy of thinking.
3. Life is not people and scene but thought and feeling.
4. The interest of life is experienced by participating and by being part, not by observing nor by thinking.
5. Thought is life.
6. People take the place of thoughts.[5]

Of course, these entries are found throughout the *Adagia* and by grouping them in this way some of their aphoristic impact is undercut, especially the authoritative and final sound that their formal elements (sound reinforcement, word repetition, concealed alliteration) and their thematic elements (predicative sentence-types, predetermination by antithesis and parallelism) produce. But this grouping shows how the aphorisms tend to play against one another. Stevens says in three very emphatic assertions of the primacy of thought in life (numbers 1, 3, and 5) that life is not comprised of particulars (people and scene) apart from what we think of those particulars. Indeed, what we think is the most essential because it is the most real aspect of life (hence, "Thought *is* life"). But this extreme position is counterpointed by what the poet says in the alternate entries (2, 4, and 6). Number 2 (in relation to 1 and 3) represents a subtle shift in attitude about the subject of thought. Rather than asserting the primacy of thought over other aspects of perception, the poet now *equates* accuracy of observation with accuracy of thought. This same equivalency may also be implied in number 4, but here his primary concern is to assert that there is something called the "interest of life" which can be "experienced" immediately only by "participating and being part," not by observing or by thinking. And it is this attitude which prevails in number 6, which seems to say that people are more important than thought. Together, numbers 2, 4, and 6 suggest a movement toward an altogether different attitude about the relationship between thought and life than that expressed by numbers 1, 3, and 5. It is as if the speaker is of two minds about his subject. Yet the contradictions produced by grouping the aphorisms in this systematic way are not produced when they are read as they appear in the *Adagia*. There they are in no such order and are, moreover, separated by several hundred other entries, each addressed in its own way (like these entries) to the relationship of the self and the objective world, the imagination and reality. Taken as a whole, the entries produce in the reader a sense that they are related contrapuntally in that they complement or complete rather than oppose one another. Such a relationship is expressive of Stevens's primary aim both as aphorist and poet: to present himself as imaginative man reflecting upon his ideas, penetrating through them to expose their tentativeness (and that of all ideas), and yet at the same time affirming the paradoxical whole that can be mediated from such fragments.

The overall relationship between Stevens's theory of imaginative expression and this aphoristic mode might be described in this way: aphorisms have an affinity with the fragmentlike nature of experience. We experience ideas and even sensations in pieces. These pieces are neither all alike or all unlike; instead their relationship varies along a continuum between similarity and opposition. The tendency to experience life as fragments is, on the one hand, a *centripetal* tendency akin to aphoristic expression in that in each case one momentarily pulls experience into a self-contained unit. For Stevens, however, such moments invariably give rise to other, different moments of the same sort and to a continuous interaction among them. This tendency to experience life as a complex series of interacting congeries leads Stevens to refuse final commitment to any one group of fragments, like or unlike. The result of the tendency is *centrifugal,* an encompassing of the plentitude of experience in all its contradictory fullness. Thus, whereas one ordinarily thinks of aphoristic expression as restricting the flux of experience, in Stevens's case it becomes the means of participating in that flux with a maximum of consciousness.

Fifteen years before the *Adagia,* Stevens had not yet become an aphorist in his own right but had just emerged from a long period of studying the aphorisms of others and experimenting with various kinds of his own. His first published poems in the early teens were the poem-suites to be examined here as the very beginnings of his search for adequate aphoristic expression. Unfortunately, the poem-suites have not been recognized for the place they play in Stevens's poetic development primarily because of the inferiority of their individual poems. A. Walton Litz notes, for example, that they "are not at all consonant with Stevens' work in 1914" and questions Stevens's purpose in submitting "Carnet" as well as "Phases" during a time when he was "well on his way toward modernizing his own poetic style."[6]

Certainly very little of the temperament and style associated with the *Harmonium* poems is immediately manifest in the first suite, "Carnet du Voyage"; but the overall structural conception is suggestive of Stevens's earliest attempt to give full expression to the contrary elements of experience. As one moves through the individual poems there is almost no apparent statement. Rather the theme of the variousness of experience is implicitly carried by the imagery:

I

An odor from a star
Comes to my fancy, slight,
Tenderly spiced and gay,
As if a seraph's hand
Unloosed the fragrant silks
Of some sultana, bright
In her soft sky. And pure
It is, and excellect,
As if a seraph's blue
Fell, as a shadow falls,
And his warm body shed
Sweet exhalations, void
Of our despised decay.

II

One More Sunset

The green goes from the corn,
The blue from all the lakes,
And the shadows of the mountains mingle
        in the sky.

Far off, the still bamboo
Grows green; the desert pool
Turns gaudy turquoise for the chanting caravan.

The changing green and blue
Flow round the changing earth;
And all the rest is empty wondering and sleep.[7]

In the first poem, imaginative perception and reawakening is presented as the experience of change. Images of motion—the *coming* of an odor, the *loosening* of a garment, *falling* colors and shadows, *shedding* exhalations—dominate the poem and connect it to the next poem, which extends the idea of motion as a source of imagination to motion as a repetitive pattern. The revolving of the earth makes change predictable—a sameness in variety. The extreme logical extention of this idea is evolved in the third poem:

III

Here the grass grows,
And the wind blows.
And in the stream,
Small fishes gleam,
Blood-red and hue
Of shadowy blue,
And amber sheen,

And water-green
And yellow flash,
And diamond ash.
And the grass grows,
And the wind blows.

Here the modulating colors of the fish are framed in yet another motion image—"The grass grows/And the wind blows"—which suggest the monotonous permanence of change—the deathlike continuity which sustains even subtle variations which we witness and delight in. The development of this theme leads up to and away from the two poems at the center of the series:

IV

She that winked her sandal fan
Long ago in gray Japan—

She that heard the bell intone
Rendezvous by rolling Rhone—

How wide the spectacle of sleep,
Hands folded, eyes too still to weep!

V

I am weary of the plum and of the cherry,
And that buff moon, in evening's aquarelle,
I have no heart within to make me merry.
I nod above the books of Heaven or Hell.

All things are old. The new-born swallows fare
Through the Spring twilight on dead September's wing.
The dust of Babylon is in the air,
And settles on my lips the while I sing.

These two poems are about death (IV) and the realization that change and death—imagination and permanence—are inextricably bound up in the same motion (V): "The new-born swallows fare/Through the Spring twilight on dead September's wing." In V the aphoristic statement, "all things are old," compresses the paradox—that is, all things are part of the movement toward death. Dust settles on the lips even as they are in the process of formulating new, imaginative experiences.

But man's ability to imagine anew is affirmed in the next new, but equally brief perspectives:

VI

Man from the waste evolved
The Cytherean glade,
Imposed on battering seas
His keel's dividing blade,
And sailed there, unafraid.

The isle revealed his worth.
It was a place to sing in
And honor noble Life,
For white doves to wing in,
And roses to spring in.

VII

There, a rocket in the Wain
Brings primeval night again.
All the startled heavens flare
From the Shepherd to the Bear—

When the old-time dark returns,
Lo, the steadfast Lady burns,
Her curious lantern to disclose
How calmly the White River flows!

Here again motion is the controlling image: a waste *evolved*, a sea *divided*, a place *constructed*. The second poem expresses in two different parts the tentative balance between imagination which reorders the sky (stanza one) and reality, personified as a star (possibly Venus), the "steadfast lady" of the sky who illuminates the order of earth by showing us in the calm flow of the river the linear, sustaining movement of experience in time (stanza 2). The contrasting yet balanced stanzas mirror something of the back and forth, contrapuntal relation of the separate poems in the whole series.

The young girl in the final poem is something of a forerunner of the poet-clown figure in "The Man with the Blue Guitar":

VIII

On an Old Guitar

It was a simple thing
For her to sit and sing,
    "Hey nonino!"

This year and that befell,
(Time saw and Time can tell),
    With a hey and a ho—

Under the peach-tree, play
Such mockery away,
    Hey nonino!

The casual, slightly ironic tone of her mocking song on an old guitar is deliberately anticlimactic. The poems have, after all, been "notes" (brief fragments) that one plays in the process of "getting the world right." Like the aphorisms of the *Adagia* the independence of each part is only tentative. All parts must be seen in relationship to one another.

Stevens's next poem-suite was published just a few months after "Carnet du Voyage." But in "Phases," there is even more of a contrapuntal relationship between the eleven poems. The central idea of war as an inevitable force in the world is initiated by an epigraph taken from Pascal: "La justice sans force est contredite, parce qu'il y a toujours des méchants; la force sans la justice est accusée."[8] This is the first time that Stevens has used an aphorism in this way. It stands as an "anchorage of thought," "a place to spring from"; its most explicit development and reworking comes at the center of the suite (VIII):

What shall we say to the lovers of freedom,
Forming their states for new eras to come?
Say that the fighter is master of man.

Shall we, then, say to the lovers of freedom
That force, and not freedom, must always prevail?
Say that the fighter is master of men.

Or shall we say to the lovers of freedom
That freedom will conquer and always prevail?
Say that the fighter is master of men.

Say, too, that freedom is master of masters,
Forming their states for new eras to come,
Say that the fighter is master of men.

It is clear that Stevens has not yet mastered the use of aphorism in his actual verse: the dominance of the flat statement repeated as a refrain in each stanza makes this one of the suite's weakest poems. But it is an important poem with regard to his purpose of expressing the dynamic possibility that for him war and the soldier are symbols of throughout the other poems of "Phases." The soldier, like the poet, is master of men in that he represents the force, the power, that makes new vistas of the imagination possible. It is within this difficult theme—the relationship between force and justice—that poems I and II have their fullest meaning as the poem-suite's first pair of contrasting views of war:

I

There was heaven,
Full of Raphael's costumes;
And earth,
A thing of shadows,
Stiff as stone,
Where Time, in fitful turns,
Resumes
His own...

A dead hand tapped the drum,
An old voice cried out, "Come!"
We were obedient and dumb.

II

There's a little square in Paris,
Waiting until we pass.
They sit idly there,
They sip the glass.

There's a cab-horse at the corner,
There's rain. The season grieves.
It was silver once,
And green with leaves.

There's a parrot in a window,
Will see us on parade,
Here the loud drums roll—
And serenade.

In poem I, the speaker interprets the call to war (symbolized by the drum sounds in stanza 2) as, ironically, a call to change—ironically, because it is a call made by the "old hand" (the older generation) which desires war as a means of preserving a particular view of reality. But that view has already run its course and the "dumb, obedient" new generation of soldiers will be the necessary force for change by destroying an inadequate view of reality (described in stanza I as the Christian concept of heaven and earth). War, like the "fitful turns" of Time, will restore "justice"—a just view of reality. In poem II, such a just view is dramatized as a tranquil Parisian scene. If the drum sounds intrude, as they do immediately in the poem they are to be answered with a "serenade" because of the necessity and validity of force in preserving this scene.

The pattern of the rest of the poem-suite is that of contrasting various views of war and peace, violence and beauty, force and justice. Throughout the series the soldier continues to represent the "master of men" in that, for Stevens, he is the symbol of the hero who can become the mediator between the terrible fact of war and the possibility of change that issues from it. Starkly contrasting poems such as III and V operate as aphoristic expressions of the two extremes:

III

This was the salty taste of glory,
That it was not
Like Agamemnon's story.
Only, an eyeball in the mud,
And Hopkins,
Flat and pale and gory!

V

Death's nobility again
Beautified the simplest men.
Fallen Winkle felt the pride
Of Agamemnon
When he died.
What could London's
Work and waste
Give him—
To that salty, sacrificial taste?
What could London's
Sorrow bring—
To that short, triumphant sting?

The first poem deals explicitly with the fact of war—the horrible discrepancy between abstract concepts of glory and the immediate experiences of combat. But the second poem affirms a kind of beauty that the very horrors of war produce: an intensified response that the simplest men feel at the point of death.

Similarly, there is a contrapuntal relationship between poem IV and IX, and their respective views of war:

IV

But the bugles, in the night,
Were wings that bore
To where our comfort was;

Arabesques of candle beams,
Winding
Through our heavy dreams;

Winds that blew
Where the bending iris grew;

Birds of intermitted bliss,
Singing in the night's abyss;

Vines with yellow fruit,
That fell
Along the walls
That bordered Hell.

IX

Life, the hangman, never came,
Near our mysteries of flame.

When we marched across his towns,
He cozened us with leafy crowns.

When we marched along his roads,
He kissed his hand to ease our loads.

Life, the hangman, kept away,
From the field where soldiers pay.

Symbolizing the presence of imagination as a source of tranquillity in the midst of war, the bugle sounds of poem IV are compared in each stanza to more traditional symbols of the imagination. As the poem moves rapidly through various images of the imagination—"candle beams," "wings," "winds," "birds," fruited "vines"—the adjective "intermitted" in stanza 4 suggests imagination's momentary, pauselike quality amidst the flow of reality at any time. Similarly, the entire suite of contrapuntal poems suggest the invariably momentary, pauselike quality of contrasting aspects of experience. Poem IX is a startling shift from IV. Here the soldier's perception of war does not allow for any imaginative activity. Rather, war becomes an overwhelming fact which imposes itself upon the soldier and causes him to feel the terrible discrepancy between the seeming fullness of life and its absence from the battlefield. The poem is the soldier's ironic comment on the deception practiced by Life. It might be paraphrased in this way: Life tricks us by its glorification of the soldier—its empty tributes to our sacrifices, its promise of the hero's welcome and crown of victory. Life ultimately plays the hangman, a distant, hoodwink figure who betrays us to Death and then avoids the battlefield where we pay his traitor's fee for what brief glory he has given us.

"Carnet du Voyage" and "Phases" stand like epigraphs to the later innumerable "notes," "variations," "extracts," "repetitions," and "examinations" in which Stevens will present his ideas not as philosophical doctrine but as versions of experience. Significantly, this structural habit seems to have continued even after Stevens stopped writing poem-suites about 1917. Between 1917 and the publication of his first volume of poems in 1923, fifty per cent of his work was published in groups of between five and fifteen poems. If Stevens's tendency to publish in groups might be due somewhat to editors' tendencies to publish several poems rather than an individual piece by a particular poet, there are facts surrounding his publication practices of this period and throughout his career that suggest his own choice and planning is involved in his use of poem groups. In the first place, Stevens always attached to his groups of poems (published between 1917 and 1923) an overall title which suggests a tentativeness about the poems they introduce. "Primordia," the title of one such group, introduces the poems as the fragmentary sources or rudiments of imaginative process; "Pecksniffiana" suggests that the poems of this group are the notes and exercises of a continually changing perspective; "Sur Ma Guzzla Gracile" (a "gracile" is a primative one-string instrument) suggests that the poems are equivalent to the mind's elegant but tentative variations of an idea; and "Revue" intimates that the poems are the mind's brief survey of currently fashionable but fleeting projections of reality.[9] Much later, long poems, whose cantos are more stylistically and thematically unified into one meditative poem, nonetheless have similar titles—"Notes toward a Supreme Fiction," "Asides on the Oboe," "Extracts from Addresses to the Academy of Fine Ideas." Stevens contemplated calling "Owl's Clover," "Aphorisms on Society" (*L,* 311). He discussed the word "esthetique" in "Esthetique du Mal" as the "equivalent of *apérçus*" (*L,* 469). The similarity of titles for both groups of poems and groups of cantos not only suggests that the poem groups were early developments of the long, meditative verse, but also that Stevens might have seen his poem groups as wholes in the same way that he saw the cantos as parts of a whole poem. Furthermore, the fact that Stevens indicated the *order* in which poems in some later groups were to appear in magazine publications suggests his having conceived the poem group as something of a whole in the sense that the order in which the poems occur has a bearing on interpretation—on the reader's sense of contrapuntal-complemental relationships between poems and hence between ideas implicit in that relationship.

Like "Phases," Stevens's last poem-suite of the pre-*Harmonium* period, "Lettres d'un Soldat," is about war and the imaginative man's attempt to understand it. But in its express incorporation of aphorism, it represents a new direction in what would later become a characteristically aphoristic style. Stevens took the title for the suite and the numerous French aphorisms around which the poem is structured from a volume of letters written during war-time by a French artist and soldier, Eugene Emanuel Lemercier. Individually heading each of the nine poems, the Lemercier aphorisms are dated chronologically and resemble some of Stevens's own one- and two-sentence journal notes.[10] As the title of the suite suggests, they are "letters"— fragmentlike and tentative—but they comprise a sensitive and beautifully formulated set of notes, observations, statements, and counterstatements for the poems they introduce.

The process of mediating these fragments is the role played by the careful weaving of poems I, III, IV, VI, and IX in which a complementary relationship between aphorism and poem exist. In the aphorism introducing the first poem, for example, Lemercier says, "Jamais la majesté de la nuit ne m'apporta autant de consolation qu'en cette accumulation d'épreuves. Vénus, étincelante, m'est une ami."[11] The poem is an expansion of Lemercier's assertion that his war experience has actually intensified his feelings for reality:

In an Ancient, Solemn Manner

The spirit wakes in the night wind—is naked.
What is it that hides in the night wind
Near by it?

It is, once more, the mysterious beauté
Like a woman inhibiting passion
In solace—

The multiform beauty, sinking in night wind,
Quick to be gone, yet never
Quite going?

She will leap back from the swift constellations,
As they enter the place of their western
Seclusion.

Picking up on Lemercier's apostrophe to Venus as both woman and star, Stevens's poem is addressed to Reality, whose multiplicity of forms, he suggests, has two aspects. On the one hand, he compares it to the constant visibility of Venus,[12] thereby suggesting the permanence of reality whatever the permutations it undergoes. On the other hand, he also compares it to the changing night- and day-time moods of a woman, thereby suggesting that the volatility of reality is also a part of its essential nature.

Poem VI is the companion to this first poem. It begins with another of Lemercier's affirmations: "Bien chère Mère aimée.... Pour ce qui est de ton cœur, j'ai tellement confiance en ton courage, qu'à l'heure actuelle cette certitude est mon grand réconfort. Je sais que ma mère a atteint à cette liberté d'ame qui permet de contempler le spectacle universel."[13] This evocation of his mother's courage and her attunement to the universal spectacle as the source of his strength prompts a poem by Stevens on the imagination which, like reality in poem I, he also personifies as a woman:

> There is another mother whom I love,
> O chère maman, another, who in turn,
> Is mother to the two of us, and more,
> In whose hard service both of us endure
> Our petty portion in the sacrifice.
> Not France! France, also, serves the invincible eye,
> That, from her helmet, terrible and bright,
> Commands the armies; the relentless arm,
> Devising proud, majestic issuance.
> Wait now; have no rememberings of hope,
> Poor penury. There will be voluble hymns
> Come swelling, when, regardless of my end,
> The mightier mother raises up her cry;
> And little will or wish, that day, for tears.

The female warrior—counterpart of the soldier motif in the suite—represents the imagination, whose violent role as helmeted commander of the armies of France is metaphorical for Stevens's concept of the violence within the mind that reconciles us to the violence without. The triumph of the "mightier mother" concludes the poem and reinforces Lemercier's earlier assertion that "love and beauty triumph in all violence." Poem IV, "Comme Dieu Dispense de Grace" ("Like God's Gift of Mercy"), carefully integrates Lemercier's precise observations of the intricate details and subtle beauty of the landscape and its creatures: "Si tu voyais le sécurité des petits animaux des bois, souris, mulots! L'autre jour, dans notre abri de feuillage, je suivais les évolutions de ces petites bêtes. Elles étaient jolies comme une estampe japonaise, avec l'interieur de leus oreilles rose comme un coquillage."[14]

> Here I keep thinking of the Primitives—
> The sensitive and conscientious scheme
> Of mountain pallors ebbing into air;
>
> And I remember sharp Japonica—
> The driving rain, the willows in the rain,
> The birds that wait out rain in willow leaves.

> Although life seems a goblin mummery,
> These images return and are increased,
> As for a child in an oblivion:
>
> Even by mice—these scamper and are still;
> They cock small ears, more glistening and pale
> Than fragile volutes in a rose sea-shell.

As the title of the poem suggests, our own imagination is our saving grace when we (like children "in an oblivion") are faced with our own death. "Although life seems a goblin mummery" in times of war, our imaginations give back to us a new, intensified world, a whole re-creation of subtle detail and beauty, and hence (by implication) life itself.

But whereas a complementary relationship between aphorisms and poems exists in certain instances, an opposite, contrapuntal relationship exists in others producing a dramatic and startling effect. Poem II, for example, is introduced by Lemercier's simple statement of faith in the ultimate relationship of violence and beauty: "Ce qu'il faut, c'est reconnaître l'amour et la beauté triomphant de toute violence."[15] However, the fablelike poem itself presents a stark and frightening reversal of this pensée:

Anecdotal Revery

> The streets contain a crowd
> Of blind men tapping their way
> By inches
> This man to complain to the grocer
> Of yesterday's cheese,
> This man to visit a woman,
> This man to take the air.
> Am I to pick my way
> Through these crickets?—
> I, that have a head
> In the bag
> Slung over my shoulder?
> I have secrets
> That prick
> Like a heart full of pins.
> Permit me, gentlemen,
> I have killed the mayor,
> And am escaping from you.
> Get out of the way!
> (The blind men strike him down
> with their sticks.)

The speaker of the poem, a heroic figure who murders established, taken-for-granted ideas, is Stevens's ironic embodiment of Lemercier's concept of the interrelationship between violence and beauty. In the bizarre and nightmarish dramatization of this concept, the actions of the murderer-creator (the soldier-artist) terminate not in the triumph of his new ideas, but in the retaliation of ordinary, unthinking men whose violent murder of the speaker has little meaning beyond that of blind resistance to change.

Similarly, in the untitled poem VIII, Stevens turns Lemercier's "Voilà la vie!" ("Heir soir, rentrant dans ma grange, invresse, rixes, cris, chants et burlements. Voilà la vie!"), with its exuberant embrace of the sheer life he feels among the common soldiers, into a *reductio ad absurdum:*

> John Smith and his son, John Smith,
>> And his son's son, John, and-a-one
>> And-a-two and-a-three
> And-a-rum-tum-tum, and-a
> Lean John, and his son, lean John,
>> And his lean son's John, and-a-one
>> And-a-two and-a-three
> And-a-drum-rum-rum, and-a
> Rich John, and his son, rich John,
>> And his rich son's John, and-a-one
>> And-a-two and-a-three
> And-a-pom-pom-pom, and-a
> Wise John, and his son, wise John,
>> And his wise son's John, and-a-one
>> And-a-two and-a-three
> And-a-fee and-a-fee and-a-fee
>> And-a-fee-fo-fum—
> Voilà la vie, la vie, la vie,
>> And-a-rummy-tummy-tum
>> And-a-rummy-tummy-tum.

Here Stevens's experimentation with lively yet predictable rhythm and phrasing suggests both the mobilization of troops and the comic futility of the endless generations of young men marching mechanically off to war.

In the aphorism attached to poem V, Lemercier expresses his desire to accept the nature of his fate (which he discovers at the end of the series to be his own death) and to believe in the existence of some eternal or impersonal justice whatever surprises it may bring to the human conception we have of it or despite the horror of its various forms. To this statement, which reveals most explicitly Lemercier's attempt to balance out the violence around him with the serenity of his own contemplations, Stevens juxtaposes his most highly charged, ironic poem, entitled "Surprises of the Superhuman":

> The palais de justice of chambermaids
> Tops the horizon with its colonnades.

If it were lost in Übermenschlichkeit,
Perhaps our wretched state would soon come right.

For somehow the brave dicta of its kings
Make more awry our faulty human things.

The speaker makes fun of the form that human conceptions of justice have taken ("the palais de justice of chambermaids") and goes on to ironically suggest that if we would just return the business of keeping universal order back over to the Superhuman perhaps the confusion of our lives (in which there seems to be no reasonable order) would take on order. (We could at least then attribute such confusion to powers beyond our comprehension.) The speaker concludes by noting that human rulers, however brave their commands, have only succeeded in worsening our imperfect lives.

Such use of irony is, in part, the purpose of all the poems which are in various ways contrapuntal to their aphorisms. All are representations of the soldier's bitter thoughts about the horrors of war. Yet all are written in a decidedly comic spirit, because Stevens also wants to suggest the soldier's abiding strength, his vitality and persistence in coming to terms with the violence around him. The poems give a needed dimension to the wholly idealistic point of view presented in the aphorisms. Together, aphorism and contrasting poem suggest the multiple forms that imaginative man can give to his thoughts in his struggle to mediate a whole from their fragmentlike quality.

Wallace Stevens republished only a very few single poems from these early suites. One such poem is the original final poem-part of "Lettres d'un Soldat." Examined closely, the reason for its later selection becomes clear. The poem contains its own anchorage of thought. Unlike the other poems in the suite which are dependent on the complemental/contrapuntal relationship with their respective aphorisms by Lemercier, the last and finest poem (later published as "The Death of a Soldier") contains its own aphorisms. With this poem, Stevens moves from a student of aphoristic expression to an aphorist in his own right:

Life contracts and death is expected,
As in a season of autumn,
The soldier falls.

He does not become a three-day personage,
Imposing his separation,
Calling for pomp.

Death is absolute and without memorial,
As in a season of autumn,
When the wind stops,

When the wind stops and over the heavens
The clouds go, nevertheless,
In their direction.

The aphorisms are of the predicative construction, what Doggett calls the "sentence of definition"[16] which is distinguished from metaphor by its dogmatic tone:

Life contracts and death is expected
. . . .
Death is absolute and without memorial

But in addition to a sense of authority ("the accepted verity or essential rightness") of these lines, there is a slightly countereffect of paradox or reversal of what one commonly accepts as true. This second effect is a result of the negative/positive play between the words

contracts . . . [yet] is expected
without memorial [yet] absolute.

That is to say, at the same time that these lines set up a sense of completeness or authority in the sense of the reader, their balancing of words sets up an enigma. The reader's basic or initial response to these lines as aphoristic is a result of seeming completeness in the formulation of the statements, but a sense of completeness which does not include his immediate perception of meaning. In fact, exact meaning is baffled in proportion to the way authority or completeness is enhanced.

As Stevens's ability to write effective aphorisms increased, so did his tendency toward incorporating them within his poems. Experiments with contrapuntal poems in suites gave way to poems containing aphorisms (usually two or more) which serve a units of thought, contrapuntal in isolation, complemental in terms of the poem as a whole. Thus, in "The Death of a Soldier" what follows the aphorisms in each case is one or more images which particularize, clarify, and, in one case, extend by implication the terse enigma of the units of thought. In stanza one, life's natural contraction (the first half of the aphorism) is particularized by autumn, a traditional symbol for the diminution of life in general as it is a diminution of the life of the year. The second part of the aphorism, the natural expectation of death as the terminal point of life's contraction, is particularized by the description of the soldier's death as unaccompanied by the artificial pomp of a conventional funeral—with its implication that death is some spectacular departure from the natural course of things—and hence as closer to reality and its processes than a more conventional human death. The implied anonymity of the soldier's death and burial in this stanza provides the basis for the second aphorism, whose first image is again autumn. The speaker thereby ties the two parts of the poem together by reevoking the notion of death as a part of a natural process and introducing the second image, the cessation of the wind. The second image particularizes the second aphorism by embodying the notion of death not as "expected" but as "absolute": when the wind stops, it vanishes completely without leaving a trace of itself behind. Here, again a traditional association, that of wind with the human spirit, is significant. The third image carries further what the second image does by suggesting the inessentiality of any particular wind to existence, but in doing so also suggests something not embodied in either aphorism: the continuity of the processes of nature regardless of death (or other stoppages). What this second part of the poem does to the death of the soldier is to identify it more positively, and therefore even more closely, with the other processes of nature and finality, and at last, through the final image, to merge it in the continuum of the whole of existence. The relationship here between the aphoristic statement of general meaning and the embodiment of this meaning in particularizing statement and image is what charges the aphorisms with that sense of restrained emotion which is the source of their—and the poem's—intensity.

The major points of this study of the relationship between Stevens's interest in aphorism and his poetic theory can be best summarized by briefly explaining a well-known phrase that is something of a rubric to his ideas. It is an aphorism which appears in the first line of "A High-Toned Old Christian Woman": "Poetry is the supreme fiction"—that famous paradoxical statement which for him expressed the essence of our attempts to grasp reality. Poetry is a "fiction" in that its unification of the old dichotomy between objective reality and subjective perception (imagination) is, like all such unification, necessarily untrue; but it is "supreme" in that, unlike religious and philosophical systems (which are also fictions), it leads not to despair when its untruth is realized but to perpetually new and refreshing embodiments of a reality in which we can believe for a time. All knowledge is fictive and must change for two reasons: because reality itself is in continual flux as certain as death itself, and because our attempts to establish contacts with reality are made on the basis of analogies which we create and which, as soon as they are made (through various modes of expression), become fixed forms incongruous with the flux of reality. That is to say, at the basis of all Stevens's thought is the concept of changing reality on the one hand, of changing imaginative awareness on the other, and of the poem as a momentary agreement between the two. It is in terms of such a theory that the poem-suites (and eventually Stevens's use of aphorism within poems) must be seen, for it is in the structuring of small independent units in contrapuntal play with one another that his ideas about reality are given expression. In the case of the suites, each poem is like a momentary swing of a pendulum. In the continual motion back and forth, in the tension between the fragments of experience, reality appears.

A late statement of Stevens seems to support this metaphor of the pendulum: "I have no wish to arrive at a conclusion. Sometimes I believe most in the imagination . . . , and then, without reasoning about it, turn to reality . . . and believe in that . . . Both of these things project themselves endlessly and I want them to do just that" (*L,* 710). To describe the poem-suite structure in yet another way, the poem-parts are like "preliminary minutia," the phrase Stevens coined in his proposed title for his first volume of poems. Each poem is "minutia" in the sense of being a small detail, fragment, or note. In the "preliminary"—both as preparation and as process—formulation of relationships between fragments of experience, reality exists even if it is never permanently captured or made final. Apparently because of its skeptical or even self-mocking tone, Stevens was persuaded not to use the phrase "preliminary minutia" as his title. Nevertheless, in the title he finally settled upon, the connotation of tentativeness which also dominates the titles of the early poem-suites was retained: a "harmonium" is an informal musical instrument upon which one might improvise a series of tunes. In this process of improvising parts and preparing details, reality momentarily appears.

3

There Are No End of Gnomes

Wallace Stevens's note-keeping between 1898 and 1912 led him to affirm the use of aphorism as a means of giving poetic expression an important sense of balance—of providing it with an anchorage of thought from which the imagination could take flight and to which it could return. His poem-suites were experiments in achieving that aphoristic sense of balance. They enabled him to inform his poems with thought indirectly by structuring contrapuntal relationships between them or by organizing them around aphorisms taken from his reading and used as initiating ideas or thoughts separate from the poems. Gradually he gave up writing in suites.[1] His own powers as an aphorist increasing, he began to assert his ideas more directly within individual poems whose thought content consequently no longer needed the support provided by the suite structures. This new direction took practice and experimentation, however. While the aphorism by definition tends to be centripetal and self-contained (and thus useful in expressing thought), if it is not properly integrated into the poem as a whole the poet runs the risk of sounding sententious in a pat, didactic, or sentimental way. Some of Stevens's first attempts at using aphorism within individual poems apparently produced just such a result. A month before the publication of "The Worms at Heaven's Gate" Stevens sent the poem to William Carlos Williams, who edited and returned it. Among other changes, Williams left off the poem's last two lines which, in his words, were "fully implied in the poem" and constituted "a sentimental catch at the end."[2] A. Walton Litz draws an important conclusion about Williams's objection, from Stevens's point of view. Litz contends that "it was precisely because many of his Imagist exercises did not fully imply the idea he had in mind that Stevens resorted to flat comment."[3] Litz's statement can be qualified somewhat. After "Worms at Heaven's Gate," Stevens found ways to write within an Imagist perspective utilizing to great advantage many of the techniques of the movement while satisfying his need for writing poems which are essentially rooted in idea. His success is due in part to his replacing, over the next few years, flat statement with aphorisms and incorporating these in a wide range of rhetorical styles for the purpose of finding the most adequate means of embedding ideas in a poetic context.

There are no end of gnomes that might influence people – but do not. When you first feel the truth of, say, an epigram, you feel like making it a rule of
. . . .

conduct. But this one is displaced by that, and these things go on in their accustomed way. There is no pleasure in this volatile morality: the day you believe in chastity, poverty and obedience, you are charmed to discover what a monk you have always been — the monk is suddenly revealed like a spirit in a word; the day you turn Ibsenist, you confess that, after all, you always were an Ibsenist without knowing it. So you come to believe in yourself, and in your new creed.

The five poems analyzed in this chapter demonstrate this range, and suggest the direction that Stevens's aphoristic style eventually lead him. Two of the poems, "Thirteen Ways of Looking at a Blackbird" and "New England Verses," are series of brief units. The former is a remarkably unified set of images or sensations which seem almost completely free from ideas in the common sense of abstraction, and represent Stevens's most self-conscious effort, in using aphorism, to avoid all suggestion of the didactic or sentimental statement commonly associated with that form. "New England Verses," on the other hand, is a series of expressly abstract assertions presented in terse riddles and witty turns of thought. Three other poems, "The Emperor of Ice-Cream," "The Snow Man," and "Connoisseur of Chaos," are representative of a balance Stevens later strove for and achieved in his more conventional poetic formats— a balance between his skepticism about the validity of abstract formulations of thought in poetry and his celebration of such thought as a place from which to spring.

A Poem as a Series of Aphorisms

As an experimenter with Imagist poetry, Stevens, in his earliest statements about "Thirteen Ways of Looking at a Blackbird" and other poems written at about the same time, reveals his concern that they not be interpreted in terms of abstract ideas. When L.W. Payne sent Stevens a reading of several early poems (including "Thirteen Ways"), Stevens responded, "I am sure that I never had in mind the many abstractions that appear in your analysis." In writing to Payne about "Domination of Black," he said, "I am sorry that a poem of this sort has to contain any ideas at all, because its sole purpose is to fill the mind with images.... A mind that examines such a poem for its prose content gets absolutely nothing from it" (*L,* 250). That he felt similarly about "Thirteen Ways" is apparent in his insistence that its units were "not a collection of epigrams or ideas but of sensations" (a direct response, perhaps, to Payne's questions as to how its thirteen separate parts could be interpreted as propositions embodied in the various images of the blackbird). In these statements we recognize Stevens's spiritual affiliation (if not express association) with the Imagists, whose rebellion against the nineteenth century's poetry of ideas led them to a belief that abstract commentary should be minimized in poetry. This belief led many of the Imagists to try to present the objective world in precise, concrete images. Such an effort is related to Stevens's belief that the life of the imagination must begin with the concrete, objective world—what he later called "the eye's plain version." In the varying but simple vignettes of "Thirteen Ways" he shows an Imagist concern for the detail drawn from common life in his choice of the blackbird as a synecdoche for the ordinary world (at least at the poem's simplest level of interpretation), rather than the "golden birds" and the exotic world they suggest; and in his assertion that they are inextricably involved in what the speaker has experienced of "noble accents" and "inescapable rhythms." Stevens insists that the imagination must be rooted in the real; and when he talks about the "failure of the imagination" he means its failure to adhere to reality.[4] Also, in Stevens's use of separate independent units in this poem, we recognize an Imagist's effort to express the objective world in one predominant image presented with such concentration as to suggest, in Pound's words, its having been experienced "in an instant of time." As William Pratt puts it, an image in an Imagist poem is essentially "a moment of revealed truth, rather than a struture of consecutive events or thoughts. The plot or argument of older poetry is replaced by a single, dominant image.... its effect is meant to be instantaneous rather than cumulative."[5] This definition is related to Stevens's concern for the way reality is experienced and expressed in momentary fragments.

But though Stevens's description of "Thirteen Ways" as "a collection ... of sensations" rather than "epigrams" (a word most commonly associated with "truth," "principle," and "idea") is close to Imagist theory in its desire to disassociate the poem from ideas, such description is inconsistent with what Helen Vendler rightly characterizes as his own later intellectualist remarks about the poem. Thus, as Vendler says, it is not falsifying the poem to ask how Stevens "conveys to us both the sensations and ideas behind them."[6] Her wording is important: the individual units of the poem do not consist of ideas in the common sense of abstract statement formulated by means of a gist or summary. Rather, they are sensations with ideas *behind* them. For the sake of clarifying her point, a distinction will be drawn here between "thought," the intellectual content of a poem, however expressed, and "idea," the formulation of thought in abstract terms. It is the presence of "thought" in this sense which makes the poem-parts of "Thirteen Ways" something more than pure sensations or images free of ideas.

Normally we tend to describe an image in Imagist poetry by using words and phrases such as "metaphorical," "figurative," "having a vividness," "presenting strongly sensuous and image-making language," "using pictorial scenes," and "using exact detail."[7] But in "Thirteen Ways" the imagery tends to be subordinate to syntactical and grammatical principles. These principles produce a cryptic, riddle-making language that gives the reader a stronger sense of the presence of self-contained thought behind the imagery than one expects to find in a representative Imagist poem:

1. the use of similies so starkly simple that their appeal seems more to the mind than to the senses ("I was of three minds, / Like a tree / In which there are three blackbirds");

2. the frequent use of the "to be" predication producing sentences that sound like definitions more than images ("A man and a woman and a blackbird/Are one");

3. statements that are chastened to the point of being almost circular ("It was evening.../It was snowing/And it was going to snow") or extralogical ("The river is moving./The blackbird must be flying") as contrasted with pictorial;

4. pictures (when they are used) that tend to take the form of huge surrealistic landscapes ("Among twenty snowy mountains,/The only moving thing/Was the eye of the blackbird"); or else whose detail seems somehow larger than life rather than realistic (He rode over Connecticut/In a glass coach....");

5. the use of a sententious diction that seems to echo that of wisdom writers like Solomon or Confucius ("O thin men of Haddam,/Why do you imagine golden birds?/Do you not see....");

6. the use of a convoluted or near-tautalogical[8] wording in which sense or meaning is hidden, as in a riddle ("I know... But I know, too/That the blackbird is involved/In what I know").

If these riddle-making devices in the language seem to suggest thought behind the repeated image of the blackbird, they are also devices which cause the individual units to defy prose paraphrase. It is this tension between the riddlelike language (and the thought suggested by it) on the one hand, and the absence of recognizable didactic content on the other, that leads to an effective reading of the poem as a series of aphorisms as the term is defined in this study, i.e., brief statements whose charged and self-contained quality resist translation of their thought into abstract statement because of the way formal and thematic elements create in the reader a sense of boundary. The terms "finality" and "stability" are useful metaphors for expressing how in the case of "Thirteen Ways" a series of units which have many characteristics of an Imagist poem can allow for thought and theme to be conveyed in a way that more strictly Imagist poems could not. An analysis of the various techniques involved in creating finality and stability demonstrates how the cumulative effect of grouping images in a series causes the independent images to interact with one another and thereby generate a sense of thought.

Several overall closural techniques are used in the poem to create a sense of each unit's finality and stability for the reader. For example, an immediate closure is communicated by the very appearance of the text on the page: there is a lot of white space surrounding very brief units. The skeletal or outline quality produced by the roman numerals helps to establish the independence of each unit. "Thirteen *ways*" in the title makes "sense" of the bald numbering, while "looking at a blackbird" both suggests a focus for the poem and balances in its suggestion of the centripetal, the centrifugal (and apparent arbitrariness) suggested by "thirteen ways." The recurrence of the word "blackbird" in the important terminal positions in each of the first two sections reinforces the notion that it has crucial importance for the poem as a whole; and leads the reader to expect to find the word in subsequent sections. And as he continued to do so, he experiences a sense of continuing and cumulative stability and finality.

However, these closural techniques alone are not enough to secure full closure (a sense of completeness) because of the reader's continuing and increasing uncertainty as to the poem's meaning. Each section therefore has closural devices of its own. Section I, for example, utilizes unqualified assertion produced by the nonqualifying word in the central position of the statement:

I

Among twenty snowy mountains,
The *only* moving thing
Was the eye of the blackbird.

The reader responds initially to the statement's authority of tone before he actually understands what the statement implies. Authority is created in II by the formal/thematic repetition of "three" in lines one and three:

II

I was of three minds,
Like a tree
In which there are three blackbirds.

Reader expectation of closure is initiated by the strange simile ("three minds,/Like a tree") and is satisfied by the conclusion partly because of the formal repetition and partly because of the reappearance of the word "blackbird." The closure in III is produced by two sentences which seem to operate thematically as a simple image of the blackbird and a direct statement about its relative signficance:

III

The blackbird whirled in the autumn winds.
It was a small part of the pantomime.

Here the meaning *seems* more explicit than in the other two sections because of the simplicity of the image in I and the corresponding abstract statement about the image in II. The reader may not fully understand the meaning of "pantomime," but, because of the extreme absence of statement in I and II, he has, nevertheless, the sense of having had something explained ("It *was* X"). One could go through all the sections of the series and find brilliant closural devices, but the issue just raised with regard to the reader's uncertainty of meaning in I and II and the relatively greater certainty he has in III is related to a larger, cumulative closural technique which works along with closural techniques in individual units. In a sequence like this, where didactic comments of any kind are so limited, the problem is to keep the reader's sense of closure in balance with his increasing need for explanation as the evasive statements are multipled. The crux of the analysis of the aphoristic level of the poem is to show how the cumulative effect of grouping images in a series causes the independent images to interact with one another and thereby generate a sense of the presence of thought even though actual ideas are never more than implied.

The opening aphorisms of the sequence, for example, interact in a way representative of the interaction of all thirteen aphorisms:

I

Among twenty snowy mountains,
The only moving thing
Was the eye of the blackbird.

II

I was of three minds,
Like a tree
In which there are three blackbirds.

III

The blackbird whirled in the autumn winds
It was a small part of the pantomime.

First there is a progression in aphorism I from the multiple/large image of line one ("twenty snowy mountains") to the opposite singular/small image of line three ("the eye of the blackbird"), accompanied by the implied white and black opposition in the two sets of images. The relationship between these two lines is a subtly thematic one and not initially a closural device. But the simile of II contains a similar opposition between the singular ("I" and "tree") and the multiple ("minds" and "blackbirds"), as does III with its opposition between the singular, small blackbird and the multiple, larger landscape of which the former is a part. When this motif of the one and the many reappears in IV, it is expressed in terms of a statement of the relationship between the one and the many:

IV

A man and a woman
Are one.
A man and a woman and a blackbird
Are one.

In aphorisms I, II, and III, the one and the many are contrasted. In IV, the many (here "a man and a woman" and "a man and a woman and a blackbird") are said to be one; thus the many and the one are a unity. The narrator may also be implying that this relationship between the two should be viewed as implicit in the first three aphorisms. In any case, this fourth *pensée* reaches back to the earlier appearances of the motif, thereby reinforcing it. It also progresses beyond the earlier appearances—seeming, indeed, to be their culmination. In both cases, the effect is to add greatly to the closure in this fourth section, to the closure (in retrospect) of the previous three sections, and, consequently, to the closure of the poem as a whole up to this point.

Thus, in addition to the riddle-making devices used in these four sections, which seem to point to thoughts behind the repeated images of the blackbird, Stevens achieves the same effect by employing the device of predetermination by setting up and then confirming the reader's expectation. It is by means of this device that a theme—the multiple possibilities of the pervasive relationship between the one and the many—is expressed in what is otherwise a series of sensations. The reader may not articulate the theme in such an expressly philosophical way; indeed, the riddle-making language of the poem works against its being recast in such abstract terms. Rather, the reader's recognition of theme is more nearly a perception on his part of the relationship between the sections and an accompanying sense of closure in each section which has little, if anything, to do with ideas or didactic content.

In sections coming after IV, the poem's central theme is expanded through the technique of varying the dominant pattern of images.

V

I do not know which to prefer
The beauty of inflections
Or the beauty of innuendoes,
The blackbird whistling
Or just after.

This aphorism contains a strong closural device of its own—the riddlelike way it combines the notion of silence in the last line with the simultaneous occurrence of such silence in the abrupt, clipped, four syllables of the line. But important to the cumulative closural devices in the poem as a whole is the way line one reintroduces the one and the many motif and expresses its two parts in terms of the duality of experience and the choice involved in that duality. Presented here is not only the one blackbird in contrast to the many inflections and innuendoes but also the more complex choice between *explicit* inflections and *implicit* innuendoes, between sound ("the blackbird whistling") and silence ("or just after"). This choice (or duality) between explicit sensation and implicit feeling reappears, further developed, in the succeeding section where it works in conjunction with the one and the many theme to heighten closure:

VI

Icicles filled the long window
With barbaric glass.
The shadow of the blackbird
Crossed it to and fro.
The mood
Traced in the shadow
An indecipherable cause.

The first four lines present an explicit winter scene while the last three lines present its implicit effect on the speaker—the indecipherable atmosphere, the implicit mood, which is half-felt and incapable of precise language.

The one and the many motif again appears and is given yet other implications by another motif of choice initiated by the questions:

VII

O thin men of Haddam,
Why do you imagine golden birds?
Do you not see how the blackbird
Walks around the feet of the women about you?

In part, closure here is derived from the way the first question seems to be answered by the second question. The choice that the speaker presents is resolved in his apparent criticism of the thin men's neglect of the blackbird (and, by extension, women) in preference for something completely exotic. Implicitly we are set-up, then, for the variation in aphorism VIII of the choice motif:

VIII

I know noble accents
And lucid, inescapable rhythms;
But I know, too,
That the blackbird is involved
In what I know.

The second alternative (in what the speaker knows) again sets the singular blackbird against the images of plurality in the first alternative. The proximity of the two choice patterns in VII and VIII suggests a contrast between the thin (lacking moral energy) men in VII and the sober acknowledgement by the speaker in VIII that, unlike such people, he recognizes and appreciates the desirable presence of the real in the ideal.

When the dominating motif of the one and many appears for a ninth time it takes the form (as it did in IV) of a more direct statement of the relationship of the two parts of the motif:

IX

When the blackbird flew out of sight,
It marked the edge
Of *one of many* circles.

Recall how in I through III the contrast between the one and many culminated in a statement of unity in IV. Now sections V through VIII, with their various ramifications of the more general duality of experience (the explicit and the implicit, the exotic and the commonplace), culminate in much the same idea in IX, where the many (expressed as "circles") are said to be defined ("marked") by the one. Here, the singular epitomizes the multiple so that the one and the many are again aspects of a unity.

In the next two sections, the pattern of the one blackbird in a multiple setting is suddenly reversed: a green light is the backdrop for flying blackbirds in X, and a shadow of a glass coach is mistaken for blackbirds in XI:

X

At the sight of the blackbirds
Flying in a green light,
Even the bawds of euphony
Would cry out sharply.

XI

He rode over Connecticut
In a glass coach.
Once, a fear pierced him,
In that he mistook
The shadow of his equipage
For blackbirds.

While there are not express choice patterns here, the reader recognizes as a pattern the dichotomy suggested between the ideal/exotic and the real/commonplace which appeared earlier in the VII and VIII sequence. There is also a celebration of the mixture of the ideal and the real in X and an assertion of the real as the base for the ideal in XI. We also see an ironic attack on those who decry the real (in X) or fear it (in XI), comparable to VII's attack on those who idealize it. This antagonism toward those who in some way oppose the real contrasts with the attitude of positive affirmation of the real which prevails in most sections of the poem.

The last two sections (XII and XIII) return to this latter attitude. They also move back toward the method of juxtaposing the one and the many which prevailed in the first nine sections of the poem. In both there is only one blackbird:

XII

The river is moving.
The blackbird must be flying.

XIII

It was evening all afternoon.
It was snowing
And it was going to snow.
The blackbird sat
In the cedar-limbs.

Section XII differs from any other in the poem in its juxtaposition of a single blackbird against another single natural phenomenon. But this single phenomenon, the river, is a synecdoche for the whole of nature and its "moving" for the renewed movements of the larger forces of nature in spring. The juxtaposition of the river with the succeeding blackbird image suggests the added idea that the movement of nature's larger forces causes the movement of its smaller and less powerful phenomena ("The river *is* . . . the blackbird *must be*"). Thus, again, as in IV and IX, the unity of nature is suggested. Finally, in XIII, there is a return to the winter scene which opened the entire series; the bird's now-motionless vigil is once more the singular (the suggested *permanent*) vantage point for viewing the fluxional, multiple landscape.

This reading of "Thirteen Ways of Looking at a Blackbird" as a series of aphorisms provides one with a clear understanding of how Stevens at an early time in his career worked within the Imagist tradition, taking from it what he liked—its emphasis on words and the picture created by them—and adding to it the anchorage of thought that he felt was required for all poetry. Some years later he wrote:

Imagism was a mild rebellion against didacticism. However you will find that any continued reading of pure poetry is rather baffling. Everything must go on at once. There must be pure poetry and there must be . . . a certain amount of didacticism in poetry. (*L,* 302)

What distinguishes "Thirteen Ways" from Imagist poetry is its "certain amount of didacticism"—its grouping of images or sensations in what at first appears to be a series but eventually proves to be something of a mosaic. It is in this mosaic that the images interact with one another to generate a sense of thought even though actual ideas are never more than implied. Pound's "In a Station of the Metro," which consists of one dominant image in isolation, has no such means of implying thought. Stevens, in search of such a means, seems always to have realized that, for him, the key to a balance lay in a poetically viable use of aphorism. Between 1916 and 1923 experimentation with a wide range of aphoristic expression led him, at one extreme, to the style of "Thirteen Ways." There the reader responds to the idea generated by the repetition of images and the pattern they eventually make—an idea completely subordinate to its presentation on an elemental level (i.e., as variations on the experience of observing one particular ordinary creature). In other words, when the poem is considered as a whole, it succeeds as a series of Imagistic statements which do not depend for their meaning upon the mind's logical or rational way of perceiving experience and formulating it in abstract statements. Indeed, these Imagist units point to the limitation of that rational process in their power as aphorisms. For, even as stable units, final-sounding and complete, they do not ever fully yield to translation into rational statements.

Further experimentation with more direct means of stating thoughts—as "ideas" in the usual sense of abstractions (or close to them)—resulted in the technical bravura, wit, and riddlelike or explosive style of poems like "The Commedian as the Letter C" and "The Man with the Blue Guitar." Stevens's two aphorisms on nudity are in this mode:

Nudity at the Capital

But nakedness, wollen massa, concerns an innermost atom.
If that remains concealed, what does the bottom matter?

Nudity in the Colonies

Black man, bright nouveautes leave one, at best pseudonymous.
Thus one is most disclosed when one is most anonymous. (*CP*, 145)

Both aphorisms are clearly lesson-making, with two speakers arriving at the same conclusion despite their separate approaches to it. The true self must not be confused with appearances; what is most important about a person is the disclosure of his true self. It is this "nudity" that matters. "Nudity at the Capital" is a black man's answer to the white man's objection (in the name of decency and discretion) to the black man's going nude. The reply to the white man might be paraphrased in this way: your real nudity (your real self) involves your inner self (your soul or spirit) and thus what you actually are. If you are not concerned about this spiritual, inner self (stripped of all falsity or outward show), then there is no point to clothing or refashioning the outer self: "What does the bottom matter" since it is only the apparent self?" "Nudity in the Colonies" is the white man's criticism of the black man's wearing new and fashionable clothing to give himself a distinctive identity. The white man argues that in so doing the black man draws attention away from his real self to a false identity. The white man concludes that when one appears in clothes that are more like those of others and, therefore, more anonymous, one's real self or nature (as opposed to one's outward manner) is restored to its rightful place as the focus of identity.

The reader's initial response to these couplets as aphorisms is produced by the technical bravura—the strong centripetal force of the carefully ordered formal and thematic elements of sound. Related to this response to wit and explosiveness is a response to a corresponding posture or voice of the aphorist which might be described as "glib." The speaker's style remains clipped, detached, and intellectual, demanding that the reader solve the riddle he has given in the sparse clues of a handful of carefully selected words. Barbara Smith says that this kind of deliberate compounding of formal and thematic elements and its resulting explosiveness refers "not only to a kind of verbal structure but to an attitude toward experience, a kind of moral temper suggested by that very structure."[9] Such a profusion of technical bravura implicitly suggests a moral attitude toward experience that Stevens wants to convey. Since all reality is in a constant state of flux, he is skeptical about making assertions (none of which are permanently true); and his skepticism results in a propensity toward irony and self-deprecation that allows him to explore serious ideas in a light-hearted, mock-didactic way.

The series of sixteen aphorisms in "New England Verses" are written in this mock-didactic or mock-pedantic mode—all witty concept, argument, and turn of phrase. Certain of the *pensées* might elicit from some readers a response approximating Stevens's own remark upon hearing a well-wrought aphorism: "Could any true thing be more amusing?" If for other readers the poem ultimately seems little more than an exercise in wit and compression, its justification must be that it makes no pretense to being anything else.

As was the case with "Thirteen Ways of Looking at a Blackbird," finality and stability in "New England Verses" is immediately communicated to the reader by the way the poem appears on the page even before he begins reading. But within individual aphorisms, formal elements of rhyme, alliteration, repetition, and meter tend to dominate more than they do in "Thirteen Ways," producing strong cohesive or centripetal effects of sound marking the boundaries of each statement. These elements, together with the thematic elements of parallelism, unqualified assertion, and predicate nominative sentence structure give the statements a decidedly didactic tone. The aphorisms seem to close like lids on boxes, with a loud "click," through the use of final stinging words, heavy iambics in final phrases, and question and answer sequences.

Besides having a sense of the self-contained character of the individual aphorism, the reader also has a sense of separate, autonomous parts created by his realization that all the parts are of approximately the same length, are uniformly rhymed, and have individual titles. As he becomes aware of this uniformity (or pattern) developing in the poem, he finds his sense of closure further heightened with each repetition of the pattern. Moreover, in the process of reading the series he soon becomes aware that the title of the poem-parts operate in two-part units. The perception of this pattern further heightens his sense of closure as he repeatedly begins and ends what is apparently a "pair" of statements: "The... World *Including* the Speaker," "The... World *Excluding* the Speaker," "Soupe *Aux* Perles," "Soupe *Sans* Perles," "Boston *with* a Notebook," "Boston *without* a Notebook."

But if this pattern heightens closure it has the simultaneous effect of undermining all sense of closure: each aphorism operates *antithetically* to its respective mate. The result is a constant shift in the speaker's position; and thus strong closure in one aphorism is immediately undercut or attenuated by equally strong closural effects in the counterstatement. Thus the total poetic context of opposing statements in a series is designed to play against the seeming completeness and authority of any particular idea expressed in one of the aphorisms.

I

The Whole World Including the Speaker

Why nag at the ideas of Hercules, Don Don?
Widen your sense. All things in the sun are sun.

II

The Whole World Excluding the Speaker

I found between moon-rising and moon-setting
The world was round. But not from my begetting.

The question and assertion of the first aphorism might be paraphrased: why get upset or take issue with ideas that are not your own. Broaden your perspective. All things which exist, *exist,* including all ideas. All ideas are part of reality in the sense that they all have their own reality and therefore are part of its totality. In the second aphorism the speaker's sense of himself in relation to reality is greatly altered by his awareness of his essential exclusion from the creative operations of nature. In the relationship of the rising and setting of the moon, man perceives a world that is round. However, he also perceives that neither this "shape" nor the process involved in his perception of it is dependent upon himself or his ideas. The contrast between the two antithetical aphorisms is between the assertion that reality does include man and all his ideas and the assertion that it is not man (or his ideas) which create the process of nature.

This opening pair of statements brings to mind the familiar, rather antithetical adages, "There is nothing new under the sun" and "There are more things in heaven and earth, Horatio, than was dreamt of in your philosophy." Within an American tradition of homespun truth-saying such aphoristic expression is associated strongly with New England. The speaker sounds like a New England Crispin, inventor of pithy sayings about man and his environment, here playing an old parlor game of matching adage for adage for no apparent end other than that of variation and ramification for their own sakes. The effect is one of tension between the breadth of subject matter in the verses and their highly compressed format, and thus of tension between the reader's sense of self-contained, conclusive units and his sense of an antithesis between the units which makes conclusion impossible. If the reader recognizes an abiding Stevensian theme in parts I and II with regard to the never-ending play between imagination and objective reality, the seriousness of such a theme seems decidedly attenuated by the next pair in the sequence, with its abrupt shift to the mundane and comically presented problem of class consciousness:

III

Soupe Aux Perles

Health-o, when ginger and fromage bewitch,
The vile antithesis of poor and rich.

IV

Soupe Sans Perles

I crossed in '38 in the "Western Head."
It depends which way you crossed, the tea-belle said.

Implicitly in "Soupe Aux Perles" is the idea that one is categorized as poor or rich on the basis of the quality of one's daily life. The explicit assertion of the aphorism is that a more correct or healthy outlook is one which realizes the falseness of such a distinction. The differences between our standards of living are dissolved in the fact that we are all sustained by the same simple pleasures and staples of life (ginger and cheese). This attitude is one which can be taken by those who can afford to eat soup *with* pearls and who can therefore afford to believe in such an essential equality of all men. In "Soupe San Perles" a French waitress makes a different distinction between the rich and poor based on her sense of those differences in background and breeding implicit in the manner in which one crosses the Atlantic (i.e., as immigrant or gentleman). As she herself is socially unacceptable in certain circles, so her attitude is representative of those who eat soup *without* pearls.

One of the effects of the poem so far is the speaker's apparent detachment. In keeping with the ironic tone generated by the antithetical pairs of statements throughout the suite, the speaker does not judge or choose between the perspectives he presents; he simply matches one with the other and thereby places upon the reader the responsibility of ferreting-out the contrasting ideas from the compressed, explosive style. Employing formal and thematic elements in a comic way helps establish this detachment (in, for example, the forced rhyme and light-hearted feminine rhyme in I and II, respectively). As the poem progresses, the speaker's constant changes of subject, his abrupt shifts and particularly his technical bravura help to undercut most of the seriousness in the ideas presented. The next pair, part V of which was presented in chapter 1, is an overt and showy exercise in alliteration and ironic juxtapositioning:

V

Boston with Notebook

Lean encyclopaedists, inscribe an Iliad.
There's a weltanschauung of the penny pad.

VI

Boston without Notebook

Let us erect in the Basin a lofty fountain.
Suckled on ponds, the spirit craves a watery mountain.

If the speaker of "Boston with Notebook" rejects the unimaginative encyclopaedists' cataloging approach to ordering reality in favor of copying the poet's smaller, imaginative constructs, he also acknowledges in the counter-statement ("Boston with Notebook") that minor imaginative products ("ponds") such as nourish most people brought up in Boston satisfy the spirit only temporarily; new, larger, yet-to-be-imagined sensations ("fountains") are always desired. Linking this *pensée* to its preceding mate is the use of similar heavy concentrations of phonetic cognates ($/$d-n-t$/$ and $/$p-m-b$/$), which, in combination with the oxymoron that ends the couplet in feminine rhyme, produce comic effects of sound and phrasing.

The comic effect of the next two pairs rest mainly in the way they parody the familiar *New Testament* beatitudes in their treatment of opposing aspects of the artist's function, or (as the title suggests) how his function changes in different circumstances:

VII

Artist in Tropic

Of Phoebus Apothicaire the first beatitude:
Blessed, who is his nation's multitude.

VIII

Artist in Arctic

And of Phoebus the Tailor the second saying goes:
Blessed, whose beard is cloak against the snows.

Whereas the *New Testament* beatitudes consist of a set of different but compatible blessings—compatible since they are directed at different men of different temperaments—these "beatitudes" are incompatible, pointing as they do to the tension *one* man, the artist, suffers between his public function and his private life. Phoebus Apothicare and Phoebus the Tailor are one and the same, the artist torn between, on the one hand, being the epitome of the people of his nation and expressing its collective vision and, on the other, developing his own private individual vision as comfort and protection for himself against the harshness of reality.

In the next four (and final) sets of aphorisms in the poem, the speaker presents various comic extensions of this irresolvable tension between "tropic" and "arctic" perspectives. Various formal and thematic devices help to exaggerate the tension. A shift from assonantal to consonantal sound patterns point up the tension in the next pair:

IX

Statue against a Clear Sky

Ashen man on ashen cliff above all the salt halloo,
O ashen admiral of the hale, hard blue . . . .

X

Statue against a Cloudy Sky

Scaffolds and derricks rise from the reeds to the clouds
Mediating the will of men in formless crowds.

In heavily employed vowel sounds (both iterative and internal) and in soft /l/ and /h/ sounds, "Statue against a Clear Sky" describes the traditional heroic statue—a rocklike (hence "ashen") human image—errected to represent society's tribute to the clear, lofty values and deeds of commanding individuals who rise above and dominate the sea of circumstance. In a contrasting shift to consonantal sounds (/d/, /t/, and /k/ plosives and harse /r/, /c/ sounds as well as various combinations with /s/ which produce a *buzz*), "Statue Against a Cloudy Sky" describes a modern society in which heroic values have been replaced by conflicting ones. In the anonymity of a mass civilization, scaffolds and derricks become the "statues" errected to progess. Unlike the individual spirit and coherent leadership represented by the traditional monument, industrial progress is a value which arises out of the lower area (the swamp) of human desire and leads not to coherent expressions of the individual spirit but to vagueness, not independent and commanding, but expressive of human formlessness and incoherence.

Stevens goes on to explore conflicting views and judgments that various types of men have made with regard to the worth of civilization:

XI

Land of Locusts

Patron and patriarch of couplets, walk
In fragrant leaves heat-heavy yet nimble in talk.

XII

Land of Pine and Marble

Civilization must be destroyed. The hairy saints
Of the North have earned this crumb by their complaints.

The first aphorism asserts that in the lush ease of a southern climate an atmosphere is produced that is favorable to the ordering accomplishments of civilization (Crispin's "The natives of the rain are rainy men" in "Commedian as the Letter C."). "Couplets" suggest all verbal accomplishments, though it refers specifically to the writing of poetry; it also seems to serve as a synecdoche for civilized activities in general. The "hairy saints" of the more severe climate state flatly that "civilization must be destroyed," and the idea here is that the stark conditions of the north lead to a Spartan idealism, an antiworldliness and hence a desire to destroy that social situation which both facilitates and expresses worldliness. Stevens uses thematic elements of incongruity and oxymoron to produce comic effects in keeping with his desire not to choose between the two kinds of people he portrays. His patriarch (connoting someone of importance) is a "patriarch of couplets" suggesting something insignificant or even trivial; with his "heat-heavy" talk (affected drawl?) and ready ("nimble") couplet-making, this patriarch is comically drawn, as are the "hairy saints" (where "hairy" suggests an animal-like nature incongruous with sainthood). The speaker does not choose. Presenting both extremes without judgment, he simply matches one with the other and continues.

In discussing this detached tone, it is important to the spirit of the poem to note that Stevens is careful about his ordering in the closing four couplets with their similar conflicting perspectives. While still not wanting to choose one view over the other, he seems nonetheless interested in showing how conflicting experience or views of reality work like a pendulum's swing from negative to positive. He thus arranges the last parts of his series to show a movement from male (intellectualism) to female (sensuousness) in XIII and XIV, and from a withering scene to a flowering scene in XV and XVI. As he will express such a movement later, "after every no there comes a yes":

XIII

The Male Nude

Dark cynic, strip and bathe and bask at will.
Without cap or strap, you are the cynic still.

XIV

The Female Nude

Ballatta dozed in the cool on a straw divan
At home, a bit like the slenderest courtesan.

XV

Scène Flétrie

The purple dress in Autumn and the belfry breath
Hinted autumnal farewells of academic death.

XVI

Scène Fleurie

A perfect fruit in perfect atmosphere.
Nature as Pinakothek. Whist! Chanticleer....

The male cynic is the occasional partaker of the simple pleasures of indulgences of the flesh. He may through his own volition "strip" and submit to life's warmth and sensuousness, but that he chooses to do so and can always detach himself from it—"bask and bathe *at will*"—suggests that his full enjoyment is held in check by his cynicism (implicitly, intellectualism). Ballata, while she is not presented as a complete counterpart to the male (she is not a professional pleasure-maker), is, in *contrast* to him, "a bit like a courtesan"—a naturally sensuous person. She is relaxed and "at home" as a nude. Going nude, participating in life's pleasures, is not something she either rejects or chooses but simple something she *does*. Formal elements of closure support the antithesis in this pair of statements. There is a shift from heavily stressed monosyllabic words using a high number of harsh or plosive sounds in "The Male Nude" to a more flowing meter (where monosyllabic words tend to take the weak stresses) and more assonance in "The Female Nude."

The poem closes on a pair which similarly shifts from a kind of "no" to a kind of "yes." "Scène Flétrie" (The Fading Scene) might be paraphrased in this way: the fallen colored leaves of autumn and the knell-like sound of wind foretold the approach of the routinely expected end (in winter) of much organic life. The implication here is that the fading and anticipation of the end of the year is a quiet thing and can therefore be considered calmly and rationally, so that its regular occurrence can be viewed as a standard (and therefore academic) thing. This academic, reflective time of year—an aspect or side of human experience—is in most *direct* contrast to the birth and blooming of the year in spring—an exciting time of change which cannot be viewed calmly and rationally and therefore cannot be considered academic. But "Scène Fleurie" (The Flowering Scene) depicts the mood of summer, spring's fruit come to ripe perfection. In summer, Chanticleer, (or, spring's excitement) is silenced. Summer balances extremes in human experience. It is a time neither of raucous excitement nor detached reflection, but of full-bodied, pleasurable participation, the season of the "Female Nude" when one tempers ecstacy, puts aside thought and (as in a picture gallery) simply sees and enjoys nature's perfection.

The series does not end in a decided resolution. However, the speaker's arrangement of the last two pairs—his movement from the male intellectual to the female participant and likewise from the season of reflection to one of participation—ends the poem on the powerfully positive note that conflicting perspectives are balanced in flux and change and in the movement back and forth between extremes. As Stevens later expressed it in "Notes toward a Supreme Fiction," in such fragmentlike motions we find "not balances/That we achieve but balances that happen." And thus it is not a matter of "a choice/Between, but of."

The reader's recognition of the irony and detachment of the speaker, in "New England Verses" is important to the impact of the poem. Perhaps Stevens's first comic speaker appeared indirectly in his use of the pseudonym "Peter Parasol" which he signed at the end of the the poem-suite "Phases." Mr. Parasol does not appear anywhere in the poem as a character or voice; the comic name is simply attached after the fact of the poem itself in an apparent effort on Stevens's part to undercut any suggestion of sentimentality in his treatment of war. "Peter Parasol" later developed into a myriad of pedantic characters who provide Stevens with a means of making aphoristic assertions about experience in an ultimately nondidactic way. "Peter Quince," an antiquated Polish Aunt, a "nincompated pedagogue," a Saint with a Backache—all are various comic versions of the minor poet, a maker of maxims in an age of disbelief. The "trivial trope reveals a way of truth" asserts the myopic Uncle (in "Le Monocle de Mon Oncle"), and in his assertion he sums up both Stevens's pessimism and his optimism with regard to the limitations and capabilities of the mind. Stevens's pessimism is inherent in his realization that thought always comes between the self and pure reality. The mind orders reality and thus reduces it to what is thought and expressed and to what ultimately must be discarded (hence the self-deprecating phrase—"a trivial trope"). But in recognizing this limitation Stevens embraces a possibility of cognition and thought which knows no limitation, for "there are no end of gnomes," and thus no need for the mind to allow itself to be confined by any particular thought, truth, or proposition: "Life is a *composite* of propositions about it." Stevens's ironic use of aphorism in "New England Verses" captures this pessimism and optimism, for by presenting his propositions through a comic speaker as "trivial tropes" he both mocks and celebrates the mind's tendency to order experience in temporary units of thought.

Stevens once wrote to R.W. Latimer:

> Your question whether art is to a greater or less extent didactic is another fundamental question... A good many people think that I am didactic. I don't want to be. My own idea about it is that my real danger is not didacticism, but abstraction, and abstraction looks very much like didacticism. It may be because the didactic mind reduces the world to principles or uses abstractions." (*L,* 302)

In poems made up of a series of aphorisms (like "Thirteen Ways of Looking at a Blackbird" and "New England Verses") the use of aphorism (usually associated with the *didactic* mind's tendency to reduce the world to principles) is meant to suggest the *imaginative* mind's dynamic process of formulating small units of thought in response to the dynamic, on-going process of reality itself. Implicitly "Thirteen Ways" point to the limitation of the didactic process. "New England Verses" does just the opposite: it pits didactic-sounding aphorisms against equally didactic but antithetical aphorisms, thereby shifting the emphasis away from the ideas of the individual statements to the multiplicity of experience. For all the sententious, statementlike quality of both poems, the theme of each is not stated but implicit: ideas themselves are merely fragmentary, at best many-faceted and filled with implications giving rise to other ideas. The pleasure they give lies in their power to elicit fresh perspectives and thoughts, however momentary and ultimately limited these are by the words that give them expression.

Affirmation and Denial in Aphorism

There are a few other poems which Stevens wrote which are made up of a series of aphorisms. The longest one, "Like Decorations of a Nigger Cemetery," contain over fifty entries.[10] According to Stevens, the title is a phrase used by one of his friends to describe "the litter usually found in nigger cemeteries" (*L*, 272). Like so many of his titles,[11] this one captures both the sense of tentativeness Stevens feels about aphoristic expression (it is like the litter left by the mind) and his characteristically understated celebration ("decorations") of its value as a product of the imagination. The same tension between deprecation and affirmation figures importantly in his use of aphorism in more conventional poetic formats. A good example for analysis is one of Stevens's favorite poems,[12] "The Emperor of Ice-Cream":

> Call the roller of big cigars,
> The muscular one, and bid him whip
> In kitchen cups concupiscent curds.
> Let the wenches dawdle in such dress
> As they are used to wear, and let the boys
> Bring flowers in last month's newspapers.
> Let be be finale of seem.
> The only emperor is the emperor of ice-cream.
>
> Take from the dresser of deal
> Lacking the three glass knobs, that sheet
> On which she embroidered fantails once
> And spread it so as to cover her face.
> If her horny feet protrude, they come
> To show how cold she is, and dumb.
> Let the lamp affix its beam.
> The only emperor is the emperor of ice-cream.

The couplet at the end of each stanza is an aphorism containing formal and thematic elements which give it an authority apart from the poem as a whole (no matter how familiar the poem becomes) and creates in the reader a sense of finality before he fully understands the meaning. The elements which create authority and finality in the first couplet are the same as those employed in the couplets of "New England Verses"—the exact rhyme which sets the aphorism off from the rest of the poem; the unqualified insistence in the word "only"; the repetition of "emperor" and its ironic association with ice-cream; and, finally, the tension between the setup in the first line and the conclusion in the second. The first line, a strong imperative sentence, utilizes heavy stresses on the first "be" and on the antithetical "seems," and contains a motif of termination carried by the word "finale"—factors that contribute to the conclusive idea that what *is* take precedence over what merely *seems*. Yet the plausibility and seriousness of the tone of the line, and hence its apparent conclusiveness, seem undercut by the surprise conclusion—for what kind of emperor is it whose rule is over something so transient as ice cream? If the first line implicitly asserts that what *is* ought always to prevail, the second line apparently qualifies this assertion by implying that nothing prevails at all, since things as they are are no more enduring than ice cream.

Unlike the isolated *pensées* of "New England Verses" or "Thirteen Ways," the aphorism here has a dramatic context, important in itself, which significantly influences its meaning. This context consists of the six lines that in each stanza precede the concluding couplet. Part of this context supports the aphorism's second, less celebrative idea that reality is ruled by transience and death. The second stanza, for example, which starkly presents the physical facts of human death, juxtaposes the impoverished pleasures of the woman's life—its momentary "ice cream"—and the finality of her death. Stanza 1, however, presents human activity; and in each stanza a series of strongly evocative sentences call, in the midst of death, for active engagement in some not-so-conventional funeral preparations. Importantly, the function of the people involved seems to be that of providing pleasure for themselves and each other. The kind of pleasure they provide is implicitly sexual. The roller of big cigars calls to mind both a carnival strongman and a peepshow barker. He and his wenches, their "boys" (suggesting men who associate with the women) and even their dead friend (with her "fantails" and "horny feet") are doubtless more "used to" concupiscent curds than funeral procedures. The aphorism at the end of each stanza affirms their pleasure-making: let the usual spontaneous and sensuous activities of these people also be their activities at a funeral. Do away, therefore, (by implication) with the notion that there should be any kind of established trappings surrounding the phenomena of death. The only emperor, the only power over death, is the power of ice cream, which here serves as a metaphor for the sensual life that has just been described. Thus, because of the proximity between the sensual activity of the scene (specifically the "concupiscent curds" in stanza 1) and the ice cream, the aphorism at the end of each stanza is not simply accepting, as it seems when considered by itself, but poignantly affirmative.

"The Snow Man" is another superb example of an early poem in which the aphorism occurring in the final lines is given power both to negate and affirm:

One must have a mind of winter
To regard the frost and the boughs
Of the pine-trees crusted with snow;

And have been cold a long time
To behold the junipers shagged with ice,
The spruces rough in the distant glitter

Of the January sun; and not to think
Of any misery in the sound of the wind,
In the sound of a few leaves,

Which is the sound of the land
Full of the same wind
That is blowing in the same bare place

For the listener, who listens in the snow,
And, nothing himself, beholds
Nothing that is not there and the nothing that is. (*CP*, 9)

As in the case of the "Emperor," no matter how many times we read the poem one of its most enduring effects continues to be that produced by "the apparent concentration in the last line of something closely akin to an adage."[13] There is a self-contained finality in the way the line sounds—and, consequently, of its apparent meaning—in the play between the first phrase ("Nothing that is not there") and the second ("... the nothing that is"). The change from the first to the second happens so quickly that the tension hardly has time to occur. But as we have seen before, the second part of the aphorism seemingly retracts what the first part affirms. First the snow man sees

Nothing that is not there   [positive]

and then sees

the nothing that is [there]   [negative]

The conclusiveness of the negation (that there is nothing there) coupled with the penultimate line's description of the snow man as "nothing himself" has led Frank Doggett to contend that the snow man represents what man is *not*—"an image of an empty body, one without an inner consciousness."[14] But such an interpretation is not supported by the aphorism as it operates within its entire poetic context.

The poem opens with an affirmation in the first two stanzas of the necessity of a mind of winter: one must have a mind of winter and have been cold a long time in order to look at frost, snow-covered boughs, ice-shagged junipers and spruce glittering in light, without thinking that there is something miserable in the wind blowing all the time. The observer with this winter mind sees with flawless objectivity only what is there and its meaninglessness. This is a poem about how reality does not reflect the ego's misery. This assurance anticipates a later poem, "Esthetique du Mal," in which Stevens asserts that it is reality's indifference to us that helps us resist our human tendency to self-pity and thereby strengthens us to bear life's miseries.

With this poetic context in mind, when we come to the nihilism of the last line a different interpretation of the epigrammatic play between setup and conclusion comes into focus. Quickly, as with the separate ways of seeing that constantly emerge in "New England Verses" and "Thirteen Ways," another relationship between the two "nothings" of that line appears. The key is in the final word of the poem. What he sees is the nothing that *is*. This winter mind, by refusing to let his ego transform reality, has come face to face with the chaos that reality *is* without the organizing, imaginative mind. And yet, in the very act of perceiving that chaos and calling it nothingness, the mind that is "nothing itself" is continuing to perform a minimal version of its essential ordering function. As Stevens says in "The Plain Sense of Things," (*CP*, 502), the mind in this situation confronts an "absence of the imagination *which... has/Itself to be imagined*": Imagined by the winter mind, indifferent, unintelligible chaos becomes the no-thing, and thereby a kind of thing. It also becomes the no-order and thereby a kind of order. Thus, rather than producing in the snow man a sense of alienation, this no-thing, because it is all that exists and therefore includes him, gives him a sense of participation in reality—and even in a kind of unity—and hence functions as a source of identity. The nothing is not nothing. It *is*. It is being.

The "Emperor of Ice-Cream" and "The Snow Man" are each important *Harmonium* poems. Their full impact ultimately depends upon a concluding aphorism whose formal and thematic elements pull it apart from the whole poem and thereby give it and its stated idea an authoritative tone. Yet this independence is countered—and counteracted—by the aphorism's integration into the poem as a whole. It thus exists in a state of tension. On the one hand, to the extent that it operates apart from its poetic context, it contains a decided reversal of what is affirmed, and the impact of this reversal is achieved in spite of the poetic context. But playing against this effect is a positive assertion that the poetic context demands.

The value of aphorisms for such paradoxical formulations, as are illustrated by these examples, is two-fold. First, their authoritative sound (produced by the formal and thematic element) yet seeming impossibility startles the reader into attention and thus—by the fact of their apparent reversal of what we ordinarily think of as true—underscores and intensifies the truth of what is being said in the entire poem. Second, their affirmative/negative structure suggests both the power and limitation of making abstract assertions about experience. Stevens seems to be giving (or asserting) with one hand what he takes (or denies) with the other, and the technique helps him convey the complexity of his thought. His own comment on the contrapuntal play of the language in "Emperor," for example, points up the tension between the affirmation and seeming negation in his aphorisms: "The words 'concupiscent curds'... express the concupiscence of life, but by contrast with the things in relation to them in the poem, they express or accentuate life's destitution...." (*L,* 500).

The method of simultaneously affirming and negating an abstract idea is not peculiar to Stevens's use of aphorism in *Harmonium*. Later poems, too, will use aphorism for the purposes of both negating and celebrating the mind's propensity for theorizing about experience. In "Connoisseur of Chaos" (1938), for example, the serious argument is undercut and disguised by Stevens's use of a pedantic speaker, who—through his extensive study of the relationship between order and disorder—has become something of an authority on disorder, a connoisseur of chaos. Framing the poem are two short stanzas each consisting of a different kind of aphorism. The first of these, though not strictly syllogistic, is expressed formally in two premises with a conclusion, reminiscent of the aphorisms of "New England Verses":

> A. A violent order is disorder; and
> B. A great disorder is an order. These
> Two things are one.

The closing aphorism is, by contrast, completely divorced of all didactic content. It presents a simple if somewhat enigmatic image reminiscent of "Thirteen Ways of Looking at a Blackbird":

> The Pensive man... He sees that eagle float
> For which the intricate Alps are a single next.

In the movement between these two types of aphorisms—between abstraction and image, between idea and particularization of idea—there is implicit the ultimately affirmative, celebrative level of the poem.

At the same time, this movement also expresses another, opposing level of the poem—a mock pedantic level. This level, initiated by the overtly formal propositions is continued in the body of the poem (stanzas 2, 3, and 4), which is dominated by the speaker's heavily argumentative language. In reproducing the stanzas below, four characteristics of such language have been italicized and numbered (in brackets)[15]: (1) the syllogistic "if all" with a conclusion; (2) qualifying asides; (3) interactions of the opening propositions (or their term); and (4) the general vocabulary of argument (in words and phrases such as "proves," "Of course," and "after all," and in subordinating and coordinating conjunctions, "if," "but," and "and")[16]:

II

If all [1, 4]
    and it is; [2, 4]
If [1]

    and they are; [2, 4]
If [1]

    and they do; [2, 4]
And if it all [1, 4]
And it does; [2, 4]
    [then] *a law of inherent opposites*
Of essential unity, [1, 3, 4]

the green of spring was blue

the flowers of South Africa
    were bright
On the tables
    of Connecticut,

Englishmen lived without
    tea in Ceylon,

went on in an orderly way,

is as pleasant as port,
As pleasant as the brushstrokes
    of a bough,
An upper, particular bough
    in, say, Marchand.

III

After all [2]

Proves [4]
    that these opposite things partake of one [3]
At least that was the theory, when bishops' books
Resolved the world. [2]
[But] [4]

If one may say so. [2]
    And yet [4]

the pretty contrast of life
    and death

We cannot go back to that.
The squirming facts exceed the
    squamous mind.

relation appears,
A small relation expanding like the
    shade
Of a cloud on sand, a
    shape on the side of a hill.

IV

A. Well, an old order is a violent one. [3]
This proves nothing. Just one more truth, one more
Element in the immense disorder of truths. [2, 4]
    B. [3]   It is April as I write. The
                                            wind
                                      Is blowing after days of
                                        constant rain.

All [1]   this,
    of course, [4]   will come to summer soon.
But suppose the disorder of truths should ever come
To an order most Plantagenet, most fixed . . .
                           [2, 3]
A great disorder is an order. [3]
    Now, A
    And B [3, 4]   are not like statuary, posed
                                     For a vista in the Louvre.
    They are [3]   things chalked
                                      On the sidewalk
    so that [4]   the pensive man may see. (*CP,* pp. 215-16)

One might paraphrase the argument by understanding the comic play on "order" and "disorder" throughout the poem: The assertion I-A that "a violent order is a great disorder" is exemplified in the first four lines of III. There the speaker says that in the heyday of Christianity the pervasive belief that life and death were aspects of a unified whole was based on nothing more rational or empirical than the fact that the two were different! The word "pretty" ironically points to the distortion of perception on the part of the "squamous mind"[17] required for such a brief to be credible. Judged in terms of our own experience of mutability, the speaker says, such violent wrenching of logic and perception creates not order but a great disorder. And so we proceed to the seemingly opposite perspective of proposition I-B, which appears to mean, as III again makes clear, that when we accept *the* great disorder—the natural state of chaos which reality is apart from our perceptions of it—such acceptance itself constitutes an order because the process of accepting is a process of making reality pleasurable, which involves searching out patterns of order in that which is accepted.

    If order is disorder and disorder is order, then order and disorder are one. The reason might be stated in this way: in the course of the connoisseur's experience of embracing disorder, he has filled pages of his notebooks with illustrations of an apparent relation (or order) in things—how the immense green and blue (earth and sky) of spring are one, how the exotic touches the familiar, how Englishmen survive without tea. Such relations are not the violent ones created by the "squamous" minds of religion and philosophy; they are small, momentary, and mutable relations "expanding like the shade/Of a cloud on sand, a shape on the side of a hill"; yet they appear in the mind and the speaker realizes that their appearance imposes a type of order on reality. Thus the relation of inherent opposites is paradoxically a "law of . . . essential unity." Like a specialist in chaos who writes in Eliot's cruelest month and accepts the meaningless chaos of wind and constant rain for no more than what it is, the speaker finds himself affirming the apparent oneness between spring and the approach of summer's solace and calm. The two are one in the sense that one gives rise to the other. While A ultimately "proves nothing," it leads to B for, when we reject A, that process (of rejecting violent order in favor of disorder) is itself an inevitable distortion. B (like A) is an idea of order, a way of seeing. In this respect the two propositions are one, not (as they might initially seem) "like statuary posed/For a vista in the Louvre"—i.e., not like fixed and separate propositions that find permanent sanctuary in a museum of ideas.

At this point the mock pedantry which has dominated the speaker's tone suddenly drops away and the true wisdom informing his discussion is revealed. It is as if he has had to formulate his anchorages of thought, however, limited, before he can be freed from their limitations. In stanza 5, at the end of his discourse, "A" and "B" crystallize in the simple image of yet another relation— the one eagle and his huge, plural nest. This image demonstates that the speaker's initially pedantic aphorism and awkward argument based on its subject reflected a limitation of language and thought, not of basic insight or the possible revelations of intensive meditation.

The poems discussed in this chapter represent the range of aphoristic technique with which Stevens first experimented after the poem-suites. The obliquity of idea in "Thirteen Ways of Looking at a Blackbird" suggests Stevens's desire to formulate ideas so as to resist their being identified with the rational way of giving expression to experience. "New England Verses," with its blatant use of technical bravura and didactic posture, suggests his desire to express ideas more directly—but in such a way as to reveal the irony of making abstract assertions about a constantly changing reality. In "The Emperor of Ice-Cream" and "The Snow Man," the comic speaker is replaced by aphorisms formulated in paradoxes. Likewise, in the aphorisms' affirmative/negative play Stevens both celebrates and mocks his own propensity for making statements. Variations of these techniques are concentrated in the first part of Stevens's career, culminating in the witty rhymed couplets of "The Man with the Blue Guitar" (1937).

Skepticism is the philosophical basis for this particularly terse aphoristic style through which Stevens implies that there is no assertion that he can endorse with complete seriousness. To the extent that man is freed from his old, prescribed beliefs, he is made increasingly aware that all ways of seeing are fictions and therefore tentative as a basis for belief. Thus, as Crispin says, no man can "think one thing and think it long." At best, all man's trivial tropes can do is reveal a *way* of truth. And the early Stevens sought for aphoristic techniques to make those tropes sound as fragmentary—as "trivial"—as possible.

Generally, poetry written after "The Man with the Blue Guitar" looks forward to eventual poetic structures which temper this exteme aphoristic style. We see the transition taking place in "Connoisseur of Chaos." Here there is a diminution of the comic persona's circular, pedantic bravura: the poem moves toward a simply stated perception free for the moment from irony and doubt. We may recall that one of Stevens's earliest journal entries shows that for him the power of aphorism is related to its ability to help us "discover" things about ourselves, "suddenly revealed like a spirit in a wood." This assertion is exemplified in the aphoristic structure of "The Connoisseur of Chaos"—in its movement between the opening formal, riddlelike propositions and the closing presentation of the one and the many image with its implicit idea of the speaker's identification of himself in what he sees:

> The pensive man... He sees that eagle float
> For which the intricate Alps are a single nest.

The complete absence of the comic persona in this aphorism points to the common practice in Stevens's later poems of formulating ideas in less oblique and tentative ways.

In one of his earliest long poems, "Sunday Morning," Stevens discovered that a longer treatment of a subject allows a freedom from paradox, irony, and obliquity. In its 120 lines there is a persona, but her series of questions and answers are only minimally that of a persona and much more like simple extensions of the poet's own meditation on the subject at hand. As Stevens explained in a letter, "This is not essentially a woman's meditation on religion and the meaning of life. It is anybody's meditation" (*L,* 250). The poem's central aphorism ("Death is the mother of Beauty") is formulated as a paradox in which the idea is not ultimately ironic and sounds paradoxical only initially, since the meaning behind the terse formulation is rehearsed and elaborated upon in several places throughout the poem. The next chapter of the present study will examine how Stevens's experiments with more extended treatments of an idea play a partial role in his abandonment (for the most part) of ironic techniques of aphoristic expression.

4

A Thought To Be Rehearsed All Day

The style of aphoristic expression more characteristic of Stevens's later poetry is seen in "July Mountain," one of the poet's last works:

July Mountain

We live in a constellation
Of patches and of pitches,
Not in a single world,
In things well said in music,
On the piano, and in speech,
As in a page of poetry—
Thinkers without final thoughts
In an always incipient cosmos,
The way, when you climb a mountain,
Vermont throws itself together. (*OP*, 114)

The poem says: we do not live in a world ordered in a single way, from a single or final perspective (not even one perspective given in a well-wrought piece of music, or in a poem). Rather, we live in a world perceived in parts and in extremes—a fragmentary, multiply perceived world. There is order to this world, for our "patches" and "pitches" of perception do make up a pattern (in the way that stars, despite their tremendous diversity and extreme distance from the eye of the human perceiver, make a constellation in the sky); but it is an "incipient" pattern—always new or beginning anew.

The brevity of statement in this short poem is clearly a major source of the reader's sense of boundary and centripetal force. The reader's expectation of the ending is set up in the opening motif of parts ("patches" and "pitches"), is heightened by the word "incipient," which denotes an early stage or part, and is finally fulfilled in a surprising way by the comic personification of Vermont throwing its parts together for the mountain climber—an allusion to the first line's metaphor of reality being like a constellation, a pattern that parts take on when seen in a certain way.

But in noting the setup and conclusion structure unique to this particular aphoristic poem, some general elements of tone and style that distinguish this kind of aphoristic expression from that of Stevens's earlier poetry should also be noted: (1.) The oblique, riddlelike tone of the voice heard in "Thirteen Ways of Looking at a Blackbird" and that in "New England Verses" has been replaced by a more natural speaking voice—a voice of common sense wherein an abstract concept (in this case, "life" or "living") can be defined ("We live in an x of x), qualified ("not of x or x"), and redefined ("but in x, such as x"). This discursive, directly assertive aphoristic expression (as contrasted with the oblique) dominates the *Adagia* entries and the later poetry. Its most common sentence type is the predicate nominative sentence which Frank Doggett describes as the "reductive, chastened sentence of definition" which gives to the later poems "their special air of abstraction . . . and some of the effect of axiom, its accepted verity and essential rightness."[1] (2.) Sometimes a charged, ambiguous, or even comic tone is used in this definitive kind of aphorism, but overt irony is not, nor is there a comic persona that stands between poet and audience. The voice of the definitive aphorism seems more nearly equated with the poet himself speaking to like-minded men. In the case of "July Mountain," we sense the presence of a somewhat detached speaker who intends to be instructive in his use of the first person plural point of view, yet is willing to state his ideas directly in several ways. This stance gives the aphorism a relaxed, commonplace sound. The speaker seems to be searching for the precise nuance of meaning: the dash in line 6 and the omission of the subject and verb "we are" in line 7 suggest a pause and something of an effort to find, in the appositional phrase of line 7, another way to word the original idea ("We live in a constellation/Of pitches and of patches. . . . [that is to say, we are] Thinkers without final thoughts"). Certainly there are some notable examples of early poems in which Stevens uses a definitive type of aphorism. "A High-Toned Old Christian Woman," for example, begins with perhaps his most famous use of this type of aphorism: "Poetry is the supreme fiction. . . . " But as in much of Stevens's shorter, earlier verse, there is in this poem an immediate comic situation which dominates and undercuts the seriousness of the opening line's difficult definition of poetry:

Poetry is the supreme fiction, madame.
Take the moral law and make a nave of it
And from the nave build haunted heaven. Thus,
The conscience is converted into palms,
Like windy citherns hankering for hymns.
We agree in principle. That's clear. But take
The opposing law and make a peristyle,
And from the peristyle project a masque
Beyond the planets. Thus, our bawdiness,
Unpurged by epitaph, indulged at last,

Is equally converted into palms,
Squiggling like saxophones. And palm for palm,
Madame, we are where we began. Allow,
Therefore, that in the planetary scene
Your disaffected flaggellants, well-stuffed,
Smacking their muzzy bellies in parade,
Proud of such novelties of the sublime,
Such tink and tank and tunk-a-tunk-tunk,
May, merely may, madame, whip from themselves
A jovial hullabaloo among the spheres.
This will make widows wince. But fictive things
Wink as they will. Wink most when widows wince. (*CP* 59)

With the exception of the word "madame," which initiates the presence of a persona, the aphorism is not in the same tone as the rest of the poem (one of Stevens's most rhetorical pieces, along with "The Commedian as the Letter C" and "Bantam in Pine-Woods"). The simple, chastened and straightforward assertion of the predicate nominative sentence ("Poetry is the supreme fiction") is quickly subsumed by a contrasting copiousness of language and extralogical turns of thought in the body of the poem.

I disagree with Joseph N. Riddel's contention that there emerges from the poem "not so much a denunciation of the old Christian woman as a *defense of poetry.*"[2] On the contrary, as the title and the whole tone of the poem convey, this poem is an attack on the didactic mentality of which the woman is a good example. The woman's aphorism is implied: "Christianity is the supreme religion." The patronizing, gentleman-persona is less prepared to follow his opening statement with a defense of *poetry* than he is to parody the way the woman's belief depends upon a failure to take into consideration a faith constructed like hers but based on opposite assumptions. His primary desire seems to be to make her "wince" at the way he proves his heresy. At the end, he leaves her with a terse riddle which is the focal point of the entire poem:

This will make widows wince. But fictive things
Wink as they will. Wink most when widows wince.

It is this kind of bravura and riddlelike posture that dominates the aphoristic expression employed for the most part in Stevens's early poems. Its unraveling may contain an implicit defense of poetry,[3] but that defense is subordinate to the reader's sense of closure produced by the bravura and wit. The gentleman's clever turn of phrase, his attack on the old woman, remains the focus of the poem. Granted, students of Stevens's poetry have come to recognize in the opening, definitive aphorism a definition which sums up Stevens's most serious defense of poetry. Yet that defense is expressly presented not in this poem but in the long meditation, "Notes toward a Supreme Fiction," written years later. In

"A High-Toned Old Christian Woman" the serious assertion is completely dominated by the rhetoric of the rest of the poem, a deliberately comic and ironic rhetoric which suggests something of Stevens's self-consciousness in making this kind of abstract assertion in poetry.

This chapter will examine how—beginning with some of his early works and then more frequently after 1937 *(The Man with the Blue Guitar)*—Stevens used the definitive aphorism within a larger poetic context. He uses either one aphorism like an *epigraph,*[4] a single proposition set off from or in the first line of a poem (or canto) to suggest the poem's overall theme, or he uses several aphorisms or self-contained, centripetal-sounding units in a *compendium,* a series of propositions (usually spaced throughout the poem or canto) which gives the bare, common sense outline of an evolving thought or idea. The purpose in making a distinction between the two techniques is not to draw sharp divisions or to make categories. Rather, it is to show how Stevens can subtly modulate his tone and meaning by using aphorisms which tend to stand alone as well as some which are more intricately woven into the poetic fabric in which they appear.

Aphorisms as Epigraphs

The following very early poem, "Lunar Paraphrase" (written 1914, published 1931), is framed by a repeated aphorism which stands apart from the rest of the poem. This separation is most obviously physical. Yet the enigmatic nature of the abstract statement made by the aphorism and its simple predicate nominative sentence also serve to set it off from the figurative language and dependent clauses of the body of the poem, and thus cause it to operate independently:

> The moon is the mother of pathos and pity.
>
> When, at the wearier end of November,
> Her old light moves along the branches,
> Feebly, slowly, depending upon them;
> When the body of Jesus hangs in a pallor,
> Humanly near, and the figure of Mary,
> Touched on by hoar-frost, shrinks in a shelter
> Made by the leaves, that have rotted and fallen;
> When over the houses, a golden illusion
> Brings back an earlier season of quiet
> And quieting dreams in the sleepers in darkness—
>
> The moon is the mother of pathos and pity. (*CP,* 107)

The aphorism at the beginning and end carries the subtheme underlying the poem—Stevens's view of the interrelationship between the mind and reality.

"The moon is the mother of pathos and pity" expresses the notion that, while the moon—one aspect of reality—does not participate in human feeling or even empathize with it, it evokes such feeling through analogy and does so at that level of maximum intensity which generates religious images.

The major theme of the poem, however, is the specific human feelings or emotions evoked by the later winter moon. These emotions are particularized in the successive images which comprise the body of the poem. The moon is the source of sorrow "When at the wearier end of November,/Her old light moves along the branches./Feebly, slowly, depending upon them"—when, with the approach of winter, the diminution of the life of a year, we are made aware of the general diminution of life itself. In illuminating winter's bareness, the moon reminds us, twig by twig, of the skeletal shape that things of nature (and hence we ourselves) ultimately take. But this awareness of flux and change in reality causes a type of sorrow greater than that felt with the passage of time and one's own life. A second, more complex, image extends the realm of human sadness: the moon is the source of pathos and pity "When the body of Jesus hangs in a pallor,/Humanly near, and the figure of Mary,/Touched on by hoar-frost, shrinks in a shelter/Made by the leaves, that have rotted and fallen." The speaker, in reflecting on the two opposing events of the Christmas story, the birth and passion of Christ, finds himself in an age when the *birth* (the miracle of a Messiah and the promise of eternal life symbolized by Mary's figure in the nativity scene) no longer adheres to what men can believe; her frozen form "shrinks" inside the makeshift stable thatched with rotting leaves that have fallen from those same bare branches of "the wearier end of November." In contrast to Mary the image of the crucified Christ seems more "humanly near." The miracle stripped away, Christ's death seems closer to our nonmystical understanding of flux and change, his suffering and dying closer to the message we read in the bare landscape. The last image of the sequence grows out of the first two: the moon is the source of sadness and regret "When over the houses, a golden illusion/Brings back an earlier season of quiet/And quieting dreams in the sleepers in darkness." This final image generalizes the complex sorrow that the aphorism means to the speaker. He realizes that the same golden moonlight which for him reveals a bare scene of flux and change, a human situation of suffering and death without redemption, likewise is sadly reminiscent of spring ("an earlier season of quiet") which symbolizes a time of simple faith. The moon brings back this season but only in dreams (not in any living form the faith once had) and only in the dreams of the "sleepers of darkness" (men who prefer the illusion of faith—the dream—to the sense of nothingness without it).

When contrasted to and understood in terms of these rich images, the aphorism's simple, truncated style and effect is very powerful. Iterated again at the end of the poem, it gathers up and succinctly summarizes all the subtle meanings and implications that the "paraphrase" has given it. Moreover, it is

6. Autograph of "Lunar Paraphrase" which was originally part of the poem-suite "Lettres d'un Soldat" discussed in chapter 2. Note that the French aphorism has been crossed out.

VII

29 novembre au matin, en cantonnement.

Telle fut la beauté d'hier. Te parlerai-je des soirées précédentes, alors que sur la route, la lune me dessinait la broderie des arbres, le pathétique des calvaires, l'attendrissement de ces maisons que l'on sait des ruines, mais que la nuit fait surgir comme une invocation de la paix.

Lunar Paraphrase

The moon is the mother of pathos and pity.

When, at the wearier end of November,
An old light moves along the branches,
Les caramanches depending upon them;
When the body of Jesus hangs in a pallor,
Humanly near, and the figure of Mary,
Touched on by hoar-frost, shrinks in a shelter
Made by the leaves that have rolled and fallen;
When over the houses, a golden illusion
Brings back an earlier season of quiet
And quieting dreams in the sleepers in darkness—

The moon is the mother of pathos and pity.

the aphorism's simple, definitive finality that enables the speaker to convey an appropriately restrained, understated emotion on a theme that might have produced a sentimental poem.[5]

Stevens wrote in the *Adagia* that "Thought tends to collect in pools," a good metaphor for this practice (increasing with his later work) of introducing a poem with an aphoristic statement of its significance which is so separate from the poem's narrative that it functions like an epigraph.

In the following pieces Stevens begins, as in "Lunar Paraphrase," with a thought whose abstract language distinguishes—and thus tends to isolate it—from the rest of the poem:

(Canto xxiv from "An Ordinary Evening in New Haven")

The consolations of space are nameless things.
It was after the neurosis of winter. It was
In the genius of summer that they blew up

The statue of Jove among the boomy clouds.
It took all day to quieten the sky
And then to refill its emptiness again,

So that at the edge of afternoon, not over,
Before the thought of evening had occurred
Or the sound of Incomincia had been set,

There was a clearing, a readiness for first bells,
An opening for outpouring, the hand was raised:
There was a willingness not yet composed,

A knowing that something certain had been proposed,
Which, without the statue, would be new,
An escape from repetition, a happening

In space and the self, that touched them both at once
And alike, a point of the sky or of the earth
Or of a town poised at the horizon's dip. (*CP*, 482)

* * *

Reality Is an Activity of the Most August Imagination

Last Friday, in the big light of last Friday night,
We drove home from Cornwall to Hartford, late.

It was not a night blown at a glassworks in Vienna
Or Venice, motionless, gathering time and dust.

There was a crush of strength in a grinding going round,
Under the front of the westward evening star,

The vigor of glory, a glittering in the veins,
As things emerged and moved and were dissolved,

Either in distance, change or nothingness,
The visible transformations of summer night,

An argentine abstraction approaching form
And suddenly denying itself away.

There was an insolid billowing of the solid.
Night's moonlight lake was neither water nor air. (*OP,* 110)

* * *

Man Carrying Thing

The poem must resist the intelligence
Almost successfully. Illustration:

A brune figure in winter evening resists
Identity. The thing he carries resists

The most necessitous sense. Accept them, then,
As secondary (parts not quite perceived

Of the obvious whole, uncertain particles
Of the certain solid, the primary free from doubt,

Things floating like the first hundred flakes of snow
Out of a storm we must endure all night,

Out of a storm of secondary things),
A horror of thoughts that suddenly are real.

We must endure our thoughts all night, until
The bright obvious stands motionless in cold. (*CP,* 350)

In the first example, the aphorism introducing the canto from "An Ordinary Evening in New Haven" alludes to Boethius's philosophical treatise, *De Consolatione Philosophiae* ("On the Consolation of Philosophy"). In the second example, the title is an aphorism which approximates even more closely the character of an epigraph and echoes some of Stevens's own entries in the *Adagia.* The epigraph introducing "Man Carrying Thing," though not, like the previous example, physically separate from the rest of the poem, is a direct quotation from the *Adagia (OP,* 171). The generalizations which follow about this last poem's use of an epigraph will be relevant to all three examples cited here with their similar movements from an initial abstract statement to the immediacy of narrative.[6]

The aphorism's setup, which states that "the poem must resist the intelligence," is immediately particularized in the imagery of two sentences which echo it:

A brune figure in winter evening resists
Identity. The thing he carries resists

The most necessitous sense.

These two sentences are metaphors for how objects in reality, like objects in a snow storm, resist our ordinary intellectual faculties—sight ("the most necessitous sense") and language: We cannot quite name the dark[7] figure of the man in the storm. We cannot even quite see the object that he is carrying, which might give him some identity. This inability to quite "get at" the actual thing is metaphorical for the limitation of all human perception. The intellect (the thinking mind) always comes between the self and the external world. We know only in part, at best in a series of analogies (pitches and patches) that the mind gives expression to. Always trying to bridge the gap between reality and our fragmentlike apprehension of it, however, is the tumultuous activity of the imagination (metaphorized as the nocturnal snow storm), to be endured like a nightmare ("a horror of thoughts"). The poem, the most powerful form that the imagination takes (though also limited as a mere expression of reality), can "almost successfully" bridge the gap between the nightmare activity of the mind and the "bright obvious" of reality. Through the poem, reality is presented as a new product (like a new day) of the imaginative night, a "bright obvious" in that it is not something to be identified by sight nor permanently named in words but something permanent in the sense that we can always return to it as night returns to day. Reality "resists" one's intelligence to the extent that it remains always something other than our imaginative expressions of it. Because it is this something other, the mind can never be satisfied in its approaches to it. But reality is potentially an ever approachable thing (just as the man in the storm is a potentially identifiable man and the thing he carries capable of being named); and thus reality does not resist or evade us completely, but only "almost" in the sense that it resists our limitation of expression by always demanding our most recent, our freshest, our *constant* process of expression. And the poem must do the same thing. Like reality itself the poem must always "resist" or evade our ordinary means of expression, but only "almost succesfully" in that in evading ordinary intellectual expression it elicits new ways of seeing and perceiving.

As is generally true of the later, definitive type of aphorism, the epigraphic first line in "Man Carrying Thing" is almost completely without overt formal elements of sound or suggestion of irony and self-deprecation. Instead, the sense of boundary essential to this aphorism is created by a tension between the unqualified "must" of the setup and the qualified "almost" of the conclusion. The reader's response is to the charged ambiguity this statement creates, and to the insisting tone of the "must," which excludes alternatives and gives an accompanying sense of the aphorist's categorical stance—what poetry *must* do.[8] Perhaps most important to this didactic tone is the way the epigraphic aphorism stands alone (or, in Miles's term, "repels" other sentences). Structurally it is not connected with the rest of the poem by qualifying phrases, subordination, or conjunctions. In fact, the body of the poem constitutes an apparent shift away from the statement to a narrative or dramatic situation. This truncation of the aphorism, or abrupt shift from aphorism to the body of the poem, gives the reader the sense of the aphorist's certainty. His idea is clearly (in his view) one whose presentation needs not a further explanation but an illustration, a demonstration of the idea at work. The decided break from the isolated statement suggests not only that the aphorist does not feel required to explain himself, but that in fact he refuses to explain himself in further abstract language. Instead, he keeps his instructive, superior stance by having posited his idea in one simple definition. His immediate particularizing of it in the body of the poem is all the further development it needs.

In Stevens's later poems this authoritative or instructive stance or tone of the epigraphic aphorism is accompanied by another technique of incorporating the aphorism—that of embedding it more deeply and more integrally into the poetic framework for various effects and implications.

Aphorisms in a Compendium

The compendium, a term for a second way in which Stevens uses the definitive type of aphorism, operates within a poem or canto which moves along on a series of abstract statements, interrupted by contrasting metaphors or image-making statements (frequently phrases in apposition with the abstract concept defined in the compendium). The function of this compendium technique seems to be related in part to Stevens's concern for the interrelationship of thought and feeling.

Stevens once proposed in a letter to Leonard C. van Geyzel that "there is an antipathy between thinking and feeling": "In the last analysis, a thinking man no longer feels, just as in the last analysis, a man of feeling no longer thinks." (*L,* 482) But such an antipathy was ultimately incompatible with Stevens's understanding of a third type of man, the imaginative man or poet for whom there is a momentary coming-together in the constant movement between thought and feeling, the man who experiences a "candor" or sense of assurance that what he feels comes from what he thinks:

The poem refreshes life so that we share,
For a moment, the first idea... It satisfies
Belief in an immaculate beginning

And sends us, winged by an unconscious will,
To an immaculate end. We move between these points:
From that ever-early candor to its late plural

And the candor of them is the strong exhilaration
Of what we feel from what we think... (*CP*, 382)

Crucial to human experience is poetry's capacity to bring together and unify two seemingly separate and polar points of that experience—the point at which reality is perceived in an immediate way (the "immaculate beginning" of perception in the senses or in its simplest, common sense version) and the point at which reality is perceived imaginatively (perception at its "immaculate end" in the complex versions of reality developed out of the simple beginnings of perception by the mind in its constant attempt to understand reality). That we can believe in both at the same time is possible through poetry's power to take both and unite them in one experience larger than either by itself, a whole-larger-than-the-sum-of-its-parts phenomenon. The product of these two points of perception coming together is the exhilarating sense that what we feel is derived from what we think.

The definitive aphorism used in a compendium is crucial to Stevens's demonstration of this belief that a poem is the validation of what we feel in what we think that Stevens commonly demonstrates such a theory in moving between aphorisms (presented as the commonsense thought or perception of reality) and imagery (presented as the seeming endless flow of sensations or feelings which correspond to, and are the counterparts of, commonsense thought). For example, returning briefly to a 1940s poem, "On the Road Home" (see chapter 1, p. 15), we might now consider how that poem is based upon the relationship between the act of stating and the intensity of experience—upon the relationship of thought and feeling. There, aphorisms in a compendium receive strong boundary by being introduced as the thing *said*. Each is set off by quotation marks from the images which follow—images which are produced by and dependent upon the thing "said." The four stated aphorisms have primarily to do with the denial that parts go into the making of larger wholes, that there is a Truth which is the final product of amassed smaller truths: the multiplicity of the world is not to be understood in relationship to some larger abstract, final truth. The three sets of images which occur outside the boundaries of these statements, but which are elicited by them, seem in turn to transform the stated denials into a single affirmation expressed directly near the end of the poem: "The world must be measured by eye": the world must be perceived directly through commonplace, concrete experience; it must be measured by the small parts that the finite "eye" sees and the mind gives expression to. The relationship between the aphorisms (as they work toward this affirmation) and the images which accompany them is clear. As a consequence of stating (or saying) the thought that the old idea of unity is untrue, the speaker experiences individual things (the single fox, the grape cluster, the tree, the night, and the air's fragrance) with more intensity and, paradoxically, as having more harmony with one another. Each image is a precipitation of feeling and thinking through the necessary initiating *thought,* the said thing. Hence the compendium formula of the poem: "It was when I *said . . .* You *said . . .* It was when I *said . . .* It was when you *said . . .* It was at that time [of *saying* these things]" that the separate parts of reality came together, were made fuller, rounder, more intense—were felt to be true.

Similar "to say" motifs are common in Stevens's poems for marking-off aphoristic boundaries and implying a causal relationship between the act of stating thought aphoristically and the intensity of feeling which follows, as in the last two stanzas of "Sailing After Lunch":

> It is least what one ever sees.
> It is only the way one feels, to say
> Where my spirit is I am,
> To say the light wind worries the sail,
> To say the water is swift today,
>
> To expunge all people and be a pupil
> Of the gorgeous wheel and so to give
> That slight transcendence to the dirty sail,
> By light, the way one feels, sharp white,
> And then rush brightly through the summer air. (*CP,* 120)

The aphorism defining a new romanticism for the modern age ("It is least what one ever sees. / It is only the way one feels") is not a tenet one would expect to be embraced by Stevens, who elsewhere celebrates the "eye's plain version" and tends to doubt the validity of pure feeling as implied in his comment to van Geyzel ("a man of feeling no longer thinks"). But this reversal of what we ordinarily think of as true in Stevensian theory might be paraphrased as follows. True romanticism is least what we ever see in the sense that beyond ourselves there is no inherent order to reality that we can ever perceive directly. We make contact with it only by our "feeling," but to feel is "to say": we give order to reality through the language that our feelings produce. Thus, true romance is the process of coming in contact with reality through what we say, in the sense that the closest we can come to actuality is through making simple assertions of relationships between our feelings and the particulars of things as they are. Stevens makes this point by means of the initiating flat statements *and* the movement from these to a series of sensations in which he gets as far away from abstraction as the language will allow. Together, the two flat statements present the discursive definition (It is not X but Y). Then the second statement, the positive half of the definition which asserts what true romanticism *is*, is particularized in two ways: initially, in three "to say" phrases (abstractly in the first of these, imagistically in the others), then in three infinitive phrases involving not saying but doing ("expunge," "give," "rush") and which therefore are more purely imagistic and more purely embodiments of feeling. The climax of these three phrases comes in the last one ("rush") where the omission of the "to" before the verb has the effect of freeing it from the static—and abstract— quality the infinitives have in the other phrases because of the "to" and thus enables it to function more dynamically, even though technically it remains an infinitive. This greater, or seemingly greater, verbal quality also enables the whole phrase to present feeling with greater purity and fullness than the admixture of the abstract "to" permits not only to the earlier phrases but to the rest of the two stanzas.[9]

Another early poem, "Anecdote of Men by the Thousands" (1918) is structured by the compendium of aphorisms:

> The soul, he said, is composed
> Of the external world.
>
> There are men of the East, he said,
> Who are the East.
> There are men of a province
> Who are that province.
> There are men of a valley
> Who are that valley.
>
> There are men whose words
> Are as natural sounds
> Of their places
>
> As the crackle of toucans
> In the place of toucans.
>
> The mandoline is the instrument
> Of a place.
>
> Are there mandolines of western mountains?
> Are there mandolines of northern moonlight?
>
> The dress of a woman of Lhassa,
> In its place,
> Is an invisible element of that place
> Made visible. (*CP*, 51)

This poem consists of a succession of statements which explore and expand the opening abstract idea that "the particulars of man's world determine his nature"[10] (or, "man's soil is his intelligence," to use Crispin's words). The statements themselves vary in the extent to which they meet the requirement of the definition of aphorism as a statement whose charged quality resists the translation of its ideas into other elements. However, even the most seemingly abstract statement, "There are men whose words are as natural sounds of their places," is moved toward aphorism by the example given in the next two lines, with the onomatopoeia in "crackle," "toucans" and the consonance of the "k" sound in those two words (heightened by the repetition of "toucans"), in the self-contained quality of the statement which its isolation as a separate stanza gives it, the use of predicate nominative sentence structure, and the fact that both of these last two elements characterize all the other statements in the poem. Other repetitions further charge even this apparently least aphoristic statement. By contrast the first statement-stanza is obviously an aphorism by the proposed definition and the last is climactically aphoristic in form as well as the climactic expression of the poem's theme.

Actually, when the poem is considered as a whole, it reveals a structural progression in its statements which contributes to its entire idea. The formal-sounding proposition of stanza 1 and its first exemplification in stanza 2 use unqualified predicate nominative sentence structure, abstract language, an assertive, authoritative "he said" motif, and a mechanical cataloging of examples which repeat the phrase "There are men" and the objects "East," "province," and "valley." But then, as if as a result of having "said" these things—of having begun a process of articulating an idea and thinking it through—the language of the speaker becomes increasingly figurative and image-making. As he works toward the fullest realization of his anchorage of thought, his examples become more and more particularized and with each particularization the idea of the opening proposition is expanded.

First there is the movement within the catalog in stanza 2 from the very general ("East") to the more local ("province.... valley"); then stanza 3 uses a more specific example of the opening proposition: man's language reflects the natural sounds of his surroundings (note the use, in stanza 3, of figurative language as opposed to the abstract language of stanzas 1 and 2); in stanzas 4 and 5 a synecdoche for man (the mandoline) replaces the generic "men" used in stanzas 2 and 3; and these lines move the poem to a richer example of the opening proposition: music, a symbol for imaginative expression, is a source not only of the reflective relationship of self and external world but of reflexive, harmonious, and interacting relationship of self and external world. This reflexive relationship is given further expression in the last stanza. If the soul is composed of the external world, the woman's dress demonstrates that phenomenon and more: her dress gives some otherwise "invisible" (inexpressible) element of that world a visible embodiment. Thus the woman participates in her external world and gives it form as it gives form to her—an idea that greatly expands the implication of the opening proposition. In these various expressions of the opening idea of the poem, there has also been a subtle shift in perspective. The poem has moved from an abstract concept, an implicitly religious notion of the relationship between the external world and the "soul," to a concrete statement (which makes no such religious assumptions) of the interaction of a "woman" and her surroundings.

The compendium movement in this poem is similar to the movement in "Connoissieur of Chaos," from flat statement to a charged aphorism in the final stanza which resists translation into other statements, whose idea is self-contained and yet inclusive of all of the poem. As the "he said" and the mechanical cataloging is abandoned, as the imagery becomes more particularized and enriched with implication, it is as if the speaker (as in "Sailing After Lunch") is gradually freed from the restriction of language, as if, in the process of expressing his thought, he enters into the experience of that thought in order to realize its fullest meaning. Just as Crispin is led from propositions to immediate experience, and just as the speaker of "New England Verses" is led back and forth between propositions, so in this poem—and all those using the compendium technique—the ideas of the propositions are not so important as what they help the speaker realize. As soon as the proposition, "The soul... is composed/Of the external world," is formulated, the mind begins to play on it; and by the end of the poem an alternative proposition is implied: "the external world is composed by us."[11]

Combined Use of Epigraphs and Compendiums

The two principal ways of using aphorisms, defined as both epigraphs and as parts of compendium structures, work together in the later long poems to give them their meditative style and together account most precisely for what Northrop Frye describes as poetry which is seemingly based on ideas but whose ideas, rather than being presented for their specific content, are presented to represent "the experience of thinking."[12] In at least one manuscript found among his papers there is evidence that, for Stevens, the first stage in writing a poem involved a step by step process of developing the bare, common sense idea which comprised his poetic experience at its inception—"the experience of thinking." The poem was to have been called "Abecedarium of Finesoldier":

I

I am bound by the will of other men.

II

Only one purpose exists but it is not mine

III

I must impale myself on reality

IV

Invisible fate becomes visible

V

Cry out against the commander so that I obey

VI

In the uproar of cymbals I stand still

VII

They are equally hapless in the contagion innate in their numbers

VIII

The narrative stops.... Good-bye to the narration.

IX

As great as a javelin, as futile, as old

X

But did he have any value as a person   (*OP,* XXIV)

One of the last pieces on which he may have worked before his death in 1955, this skeleton plan for "Abecedarium of Finesoldier" provides us with a clue as to how Stevens first conceived and proceeded to write a poem. The title, full blown and probably thought of first,[13] contains the suggestion of so many of his titles that we perceive reality in parts or fragments, as "notes" or "phases," and implies that what follows are the rudiments, the ABC's, of tracing an idea through various ramifications, feelings, and sensations. Important for the purposes of this study is the evidence here that the entire poem was initially conceived in a series of brief statements. It is not known, of course, how many of Stevens's poems were first thought-out in this aphoristic, outline form. His numerous notebooks (including *Adagia* and one called "Skemata," which contains proposed first lines and titles) would seem to indicate that the exercise of getting down the initial experience of the poem as a set of anchorages of thought may have been a fairly standard procedure. After all, to start with an idea, and then to give it to the mind for full play, to rehearse it, exercise it, to move away from and return to it, to let the mind play with inexhaustible ways of expressing and discovering more about it—that, for Stevens, was the process called poetry or the "supreme fiction." Characteristically, a poem fully developed into cantos still seems to work in outline fashion to give the reader the sense of how poetry is a continual movement from idea to feeling and sensation and back to idea again.

For example, if we isolate the aphoristic units from the first four cantos of "An Ordinary Evening in New Haven," we get a clear sense of Stevens's desire to give the reader a representation of the poetic process of moving through changes of perspective and arriving at new understandings as thought moves to larger thought and back again in a continual turning and revolving of an initial idea. Each aphorism is used to initiate its canto much as an epigraph would, but in the context of the poem as a whole these seeming epigraphs work as parts of a compendium—as various aspects or stages of a developing idea which operate to link the cantos together:

> The eye's plain version is a thing apart,
> A vulgate of experience. (I)

>   ... we cannot tell apart
> The idea and the bearer-being of the idea. (II)

> The point of vision and desire are the same. (III)

> The plainness of plain things is savagery (IV)[14]

Looked at in close proximity, these aphorisms suggest that the speaker is of several minds about his subject. Aphorism I says that the common version of experience (or reality) is the version received through what one sees (or experiences physically, immediately through the sense perception as opposed, presumably, to versions received more intellectually), and that this version is a "thing apart"—unique, valuable all by itself, not dependent upon other versions. II and III qualify this idea tremendously. II says that we cannot tell apart the "idea" (the mind's conception of reality) from the "bearer-being of idea" (the inevitably biased nature of the mind which has the conception). III is a further development of this thought: we cannot separate what we see (the point of "vision," the eye's plain version of experience, the point of immediate or common sense perception) from what we want to see (the point of "desire"); that is, sense perception is filtered through the mind, and the mind's desire for a particular version of reality affects how the eye interprets reality for the mind and vice versa. Finally, recalling the truth of aphorism I, that the eye's plain version is a thing apart, aphorism IV returns to that propositon—but with a development in a new direction: "The plainness of plain things is savagery"—plainness is not the simple and easy thing it seems to be but the effect and cause of great savagery.[15] Within the four-part series of these cantos, then, the epigraphic aphorism (used in three instances) to introduce a canto with a seemingly isolated, independent thought) also serves the dual function of being part of a compendium and is thus representative of a particular turn of a thought presented in the previous canto.

The removal of the aphorisms in the poem from their contexts and the study of them simply in relationship to each other has brought out certain recurrent characteristics of Stevens's use of aphorisms discussed earlier with regard to the *Adagia,* the poem-suites, and the poems comprised of a series of aphorisms. In a way similar to the contrapuntal relationship of the entries in the *Adagia,* the aphorisms in cantos II, III, and IV only seem to oppose the aphorism in I. Ultimately they complement it: the eye's plain version can be and is the commonly received view of reality, unique and valuable in and of itself. (Such plainness is never easily arrived at or maintained, but always the result or cause of a complementary violence or savagery of feeling.) At the same time it is equally true that the mind's desire for a certain idea of reality is also a thing apart, a unique and valuable version of reality. Finally, it is also true that we cannot easily separate the eye's version from the mind's version.

In the poem-suites, a comparable contrapuntal relationship was presented in the juxtapositioning of contrasting poems to suggest (rather than state, as Stevens does in the canto aphorisms) opposing views of experience corresponding to Stevens's view of reality as a constant process of flux and change. In poems comprised of aphorisms used in a series, such as "New England Verses,"[16] the finality and authority of each particular idea presented was undercut by the use of witty antithesis and an ironic speaker. Within a series of cantos the process of one definitive statement giving way to another creates a poetic structure which enables Stevens to convey to the reader an even more immediate and continuous sense of the seemingly endless approaches to and directions away from an idea. Stevens's own phrase from "An Ordinary Evening in New Haven" (consisting of 31 cantos)—"A thought to be rehearsed all day"—is an apt metaphor for this canto structure and the resulting reader experience.

Below are eight aphorisms in "An Ordinary Evening in New Haven," listed in the order in which they appear after the aphorisms of the first four cantos:

Reality as a thing seen by the mind
Not that which is but that which is apprehended. (V)

Reality is the beginning not the end. (VI)

That which was incredible becomes... credible day again. (VII)

We keep coming back and coming back
To the real. (IX)

We do not know what is real and what is not. (X)

The search for
Reality is as momentous as the search for God. (XXII)

If it should be true that reality exists in the
mind... then it follows that the real and the unreal are two in one. (XXVIII)

It is not an empty clearness, a bottomless sight
It is a visibility of thought
In which hundreds of eyes, in one mind, see at once. (XXX)

The speaker continues to explore the paradoxical nature of reality as both a thing apart from the imagination (or the mind) and a thing dependent upon it. On the one hand, V defines reality exclusively as what the mind apprehends. But VI, VII, and IX each imply the opposing perspective: VI asserts that the real is the base of perception—the "beginning" or plain version of things, something apart from the mind (although certainly not a final, fixed thing or "end"). Likewise VII identifies reality with this vulgate or plain version, the credible fact to which the mind's incredible (desired) version must return; and similarly IX implies that the real is something apart from the mind in its assertion that the mind, in its desire for reality to be a certain way, must repeatedly come back to what reality is apart from desire. But then X "resolves" the contradiction posed in juxtaposing the two views (reality as a thing apart and a thing apprehended) by asserting that the whole problem is not resolvable. Interrupting the back and forth nature of these assertions are neutral ones like XXII which, rather than addressing itself to the nature of reality, says that it is, after all, the *search* for reality—a modern search which occupies the imagination in the same way that the search for God once occupied it—that is important (regardless of what we decide reality is). XXVIII draws an inference from the aphorism back in canto V, resolving the problem of the real versus the unreal in terms of V's assertion. Finally the image of the hundreds of eyes seeing at once (XXX) seems to resolve the problem in still another way by drawing an analogy between reality and the mind. Just as reality is dynamic, so it is perceived in many different ways by a dynamic mind with hundreds of different perspectives. Reality is equal to those occasional moments when the mind's varying perspectives are compatible and come together in a single vision of thought. That is to say, perhaps reality is that brief and fleeting moment when, on occasion, the mind's desire for reality to be a certain way adheres or coincides to what reality actually is apart from desire.

7.   Autograph from journal: "Sometimes I think that all our
     learning is the little learning of the maxim."

Deceit — how inevitable! Pride,
lack of sophistication, ignorance, egoism
— what dreadful things! Necessity, too—.
I can't make head or tail of it.
Law is a fine thing, Art is a
fine thing, · Nature is a fine thing;
but the average human mind and
spirit are confusing beyond measure.
I sometimes I think that all our
learning is the little learning of
the maxim.

Of course, these aphorisms are found within larger poetic contexts of
individual cantos where they serve various functions. They are grouped as they
are in this study to point out an important metaphorical role they serve in the
poem as a whole.

The underlying question of the poem is, "How do we know reality?" Is
reality what it seems to be to common, everyday sense experience, something
apart from perception; or is it (partly or wholly) a human creation determined
by and expressive of what the mind desires it to be? The question is one the
speaker believes cannot be resolved, and he does not ask it so that it can be.
Rather, he believes that the value of this question lies simply in its continual
and varied asking. In that asking we engage, he believes, in a process of
thinking which is like the process of reality itself—"something not yet true," a

potential, the development of an incipient pattern which imaginative man "perceives through truth" (see canto XVIII), "truth" being the various propositions or questions he composes and discards. And that is essentially the metaphorical role that the play of aphorisms seem to have in these long poems—as a simulacrum of the process of thinking, parallel to the process of reality itself.

5

Notes toward a Supreme Fiction

In a brief discussion of "Notes toward a Supreme Fiction" the major points of the present study of aphorism in Stevens's poetry will be summarized. In general highly representative of his longer meditative verse, the poem is distinctive in the way its 30 cantos are formally structured around three self-contained statements (each introducing 10 cantos): "It must be abstract," "It must change," "It must give pleasure." On the one hand, the repetition of the definitive and insisting "it must" phrase establishes an effect of the poet/aphorist speaking in an authoritative and categorical way, defining the essential qualities of the difficult concept of a "supreme fiction"—what it must be, what it must do and give. By beginning with a nonqualifying "it must" statement and moving abruptly from that isolated *pensée* to the body of the poem, Stevens suggests that he does not feel required to explain himself and refuses to do so in further abstract language. In this way he achieves a didactic, superior stance of one who has posited his idea in a single simple definition. The aphorisms are thus strongly centripetal: they seem to be complete as if they are all that can or need be said apart from the particularizing of the statement in the body of the poem.

But at the same time that the aphorisms produce this initial effect in the poem they also have another, almost opposing, effect because of the way they ultimately interact with each other and with the cantos they introduce (their compendium effect). Stevens partially describes this second effect when he explains in a letter to Henry Church that the aphorisms

> are not the articulations that one would expect to find between paragraphs and chapters of a work of philosophy....A philosopher is never at rest unless he is systematizing: constructing a theory. But these are Notes... three notes by way of defining the characteristics of Supreme fiction [or]... poetry. (*L,* 407)

In a more general comment about the whole poem, Stevens writes: "I have written... a series of poems dealing with the idea of a supreme fiction, or rather playing with that idea" (*L,* 409). For Stevens, of course, aphorisms have always been a means whereby one "plays" with ideas—gives the mind free play to discover in the thought the most that it implies before discarding both thought and implication and proceeding to another. Such a view of a poem as an informal playing with an idea is expressed rather explicitly in the poem's title ("Notes toward a Supreme Fiction"), whose aphoristic implications have already been discussed. As "Notes" (the casual observations and jottings one might enter in a journal) "toward" (moving in the direction of as opposed to arriving at some conclusion), the title makes no final claims for what the poem-parts will do. This notion of the movement *toward* something (and its subtle self-deprecating expression in so many of the poems' titles) reaches far back into Stevens's larger poetic theory (present in any poem regardless of its subject) of the ever-changing, dynamic relationship that exists between imagination and reality: since poetry is the representation of this relationship, any particular poem must therefore be presented and understood as a mere stage, fragment, or part of a continual process. Moreover, in any one poem it is not the particular content that should be emphasized but the way in which this larger poetic experience of thinking and feeling is captured.

In "Notes toward a Supreme Fiction" Stevens gives this larger theory specific embodiment through a relatively loose canto sequence which, in contrast to the formal-sounding aphorisms which head them, take the abstraction presented in the headings in innumerable directions (or "rehearsals") which there is no attempt to chart. As Stevens himself explained,

> At first I attempted to follow a scheme and the first poem bore the caption REFACTIMENTO.... But I very soon found that, if I stuck closely to a development, I should lose all the qualities that I really wanted to get into the thing, and that I was likely to produce something that did not come off in any sense, not even as poetry (*L,* 431).

The "qualities" that he suggests would have been lost in a formal structuring of the cantos, are related to the balance he achieves in the poem between his abstract initial thoughts about the subject, which are expressed by the aphoristic headings, and his casual exploration in the cantos of the feeling to which the thoughts give rise.

The first anchorage of thought—"It must be abstract"—introduces the first stage of the poem, whose cantos are concerned with our approaching the supreme fiction by starting with reality stripped of all fictions (the artificial forms we have imposed on it), with how our first idea of the supreme fiction must be like our freshest thought about reality—free from all previous human conceptions. A mature Crispin, still witty and didactic but less ironic than in the earlier poetry, opens the series. The use of the slightly comic speaker at the beginning provides the most decided break between the formal stance of the aphorism and the informal "rehearsal" of its idea which is the larger intent of the poem.

In canto I, this speaker speaks in the voice of the academic, detached self he has become as a mature poet, but he addresses the ephebic, potentially fresh poet within himself, whom he tells how to begin again with "the first idea"— how to be a thinker without final thoughts, how to see the world abstractly but apart from the stale fictions we ordinarily use to speak of it. In this opening canto, his riddlelike language ("the invented world" of "the ignorant man with an ignorant eye" who has learned "to be in the difficulty of what it means to be") implicitly conveys the old poet's realization of how limited his language is when it comes to defining the difficult concept of the supreme fiction. Such self-consciousness about giving expression to what ultimately cannot be expressed gradually diminishes in the remaining cantos of this first—"It must be abstract"—stage of the poem. After the flat catalog of one-sentence *pensées* and convoluted syntax of canto I, there is a movement generally toward a looser, more lyrical rehearsal of the notion of the "first idea." On the other hand, the difficulty of the concept of starting with the abstract idea of reality is that it requires that these cantos (again, generally speaking) be the most discursive in the whole poem—and indeed they represent the barest beginnings of the thought/feeling process of the poem. Their lyrical passages are almost always introduced, interrupted, or concluded by aphoristic units of thought characterized by argumentative syntax—(1) question and answer sequences; (2) antitheses; (3) discursive patterns of speech ("it is not x but y"); (4) a formal, authoritative "we" voice frequently accompanied by imperative and, therefore, didactic-sounding verbs; (5) formal repetitions of words and phrases which echo canto I's initial definitive statement about the "first idea": "It is ennuie . . . that sends us back to the first idea" (II); "there [may] be ennuie of the first idea" (II); "The poem refreshes life so that we share the first idea" (IV); "the first idea was not our own" (V); "It feels good . . . without the first idea" (VII); "The first idea is an imagined thing" (IX).

The movement from "It must be abstract" to "It must change" is like the movement of two commonsense thoughts in a compendium of thoughts—one idea is an outgrowth of the other. Once the supreme fiction is translated from the bare, abstract idea of it to forms of thought and feeling in poetry, its primary quality is that it must always be seen as a process, not a fixed form, that *it must change*. In this second stage the speaker is thus concerned with an effect of the idea of the first stage. This new concern is expressed not only in a new aphorism but in a new formal emphasis in the accompanying 10 cantos. The emphasis is now less upon discursive statement, more on a modulation between mildly discursive cantos on the subject of change (I, IV, VII, IX, and X) and more immediate *demonstrations* of that subject in the interrupting allegories, anecdotes, personifications, and narratives (II, III, V, VI and VII). Not only are there considerably fewer discursive devices in this second stage, but within the alternating discursive cantos there is considerably more freedom from heavy echoes of a line of argumentation. Although the authoritative "we" voice is the consistent voice and there are sporadic minor echoes of it—"We say this changes and that changes" (I); "we say/We have not the need of any paradise" (VII)—the reader does not have the strong sense of a persona (the poet/teacher addressing the ephebe) that he did in stage one. Instead, the many digressive vignettes (on the president, the statue, the planter, the sparrow, and Nanzia Nunzio) give the reader a much stronger sense of that increasing back-and-forth process between thought and feeling which constitutes the poetic experience and goes on throughout the poem.

In the final stage of the poem, the thoughts of the first two aphorisms—"It must be abstract" and "It must change"—give rise to a third and final thought bound up in the first two: "It must give pleasure." To show fully how this third thought functions as the climactic outgrowth of what has come before (and thus as part of the larger simulacrum of how thought and feeling interact) it is useful to look at a smaller unit in the poem, the individual canto. For example, canto IV is a microcosm of the entire three-part movement of the whole series of aphorisms and cantos. Paralleling the three stages of the "abstract," "change," and "give pleasure" compendium in the entire poem, there are in the canto three commonsense thoughts that together comprise a compendium of the three-stage development of the idea of the canto:

> *Two things of opposite natures seem to depend*
> *On one another,* as a man depends
> On a woman, day on night, the imagined
>
> On the real. *This is the origin of change.*
> Winter and spring, cold copulars, embrace
> And forth the particulars of rapture come.
>
> Music falls on the silence like a sense,
> A passion that we feel, not understand.
> Morning and afternoon are clasped together
>
> And North and South are an intrinsic couple
> And sun and rain a plural, like two lovers
> That walk away as one in the greenest body.
>
> In solitude the trumpets of solitude
> Are not of another solitude resounding;
> A little string speaks for a crowd of voices.
>
> *The partaker partakes of that which changes him.*
> The child that touches takes character from the thing,
> The body, it touches. The captain and his men

Are one and the sailor and the sea are one.
Follow after, O my companion, my fellow, my self,
Sister and solace, brother and delight.

The first stage is the shortest, consisting of an aphorism and a brief catalog. The catalog does two things: it particularizes the aphorism with concrete examples, and it touches, despite its brevity, on three very diverse expressions—in love, in nature, and in epistemology—of the common sense of the aphorism. The next stage of the poem is again structured in terms of an initiating aphorism followed by a catalog of illustrative examples. Here the speaker is concerned with an effect of the idea of the first part of the poem. This new concern is expressed not only in a new aphorism but in a new emphasis in its accompanying catalog. This catalog is longer, more lyrical, and more emotional than the first one. It is dominated by words that suggest sensuous immediate pleasure ("sense," "passion," "clasped together," "couple," "lovers," "greenest body"). As a result, the focus of the catalog is less on its particular items than on a celebration of change. This shift of emphasis is an appropriate embodiment of the second aphorism. But it is more than that. Whereas the first catalog simply illustrates its initiating aphorism, this catalog both embodies and develops the idea of its aphorism. What the speaker says in the aphorism and the catalog together is that the single, unifying experience in the general interdependency of opposite things is the sensual pleasure of change and variety.

The third stage of the canto is again marked by an initial aphorism once again followed by a catalog. The third assertion ("The partaker partakes of that which changes him") contains both the preceding assertions (1) that things of opposite natures depend on one another, and (2) that this dependency results in the variety and pleasure of perpetual change. But the new *pensée* also adds something more: the idea of the ultimate inseparability of things of opposite nature (inseparable because of their participation in one another), and the resulting, exhilarating sense of Whitman-like personal identity with all things and thus of self-discovery. This second point is the climax of the canto, the moment toward which all the rest of it moves. Its intensity leads to expression which is more passionate, more personal than that in the rest of the poem, given form, appropriately, not in declarative statement but in imperative exhortation.

Each part of the canto begins with an aphoristic abstract statement, followed by a catalog of illustrative examples. In the second part of the poem this catalog has greater emotional intensity than it does in the first part and contributes more to the total meaning. The third catalog initially returns to the simple illustrative function of the first catalog. But then it suddenly becomes the speaker's ecstatic response to the point at which his thought and feeling have arrived, expressed as a lyrical apostrophe to the nonself, which is viewed now as a companion and even as the speaker himself.

Likewise, the entire three stages of "Notes toward a Supreme Fiction" move toward a culmination in its last—"It must give pleasure"—stage. Here, as in the last stage of the individual canto just considered, there are brief allusions to the interacting ideas that have come before: to the first stage argument about the "first idea" (how "to find the real,/To be stripped of every fiction except one/The fiction of an absolute," VII) and to the second stage theme of change (how we find the real "in difference... /In a moving contour, a change not quite completed," X). But, as in the case of the individual canto, the new *pensée* of the third stage and its accompanying cantos contain a new emphasis—the idea that in all our fresh perceptions of the first idea and in all our embracings of its changing aspects, there is something larger given and intensely felt, that is, the *pleasure* of continual new discoveries of reality and thus of the self. This last point is likewise the climax of all the aphorisms and their cantos, the moment toward which the rest of the poem moves. It is appropriately expressed by the most lyrical, passionate, and ultimately most personal passage of the poem— the last three cantos. The authoritative, discursive, and didactic "we" voice that dominated stages one and two is transformed by the sudden appearance here for the first time of the first person singular "I" voice. This change signifies that the teacher and the ephebe have become one:

> What am I to believe?...
> I have not but I am and as I am, I am. (VIII)
>
> I can/Do all that angels can... (IX)
>
> I call you by name, my green, my fluent mundo... (X)

Moreover, in contrast to the earlier persona's relatively abstract and discursive arguments about reality as "first idea," the "I" speaker here suggests the direction in which the rehearsal of ideas (or "notes") has taken him—toward a fresh discovery of reality. For not only does the voice in these last cantos become more personal, but reality itself is also finally addressed directly in a compounded personification of fluctuating earth and ever-changing woman:

> Fat girl, terrestrial, my summer, my night,
> How is it I find you in difference, see you there
> In a moving contour, a change not quite completed?
>
> You are familiar yet an aberration.
> Civil, madam, I am, but underneath
> A tree, this unprovoked sensation requires

That I should name you flatly, waste no words,
Check your evasions, hold you to yourself.
Even so when I think of you as strong or tired,

Bent over work, anxious, content, alone,
You remain the more than natural figure. You
Become the soft-footed phantom, the irrational

Distortion, however fragrant, however dear.
That's it: the more than rational distortion,
The fiction that results from feeling. Yes, that.

They will get it straight one day at the Sorbonne.
We shall return at twilight from the lecture
Pleased that the irrational is rational,

Until flicked by feeling, in a gildered street,
I call you by name, my green, my fluent mundo.
You will have stopped revolving except in crystal.

The personifications of reality are underscored as the first person speaker's *own* invention ("my summer, my night," "my green, my fluent mundo"), as *his* "irrational distortion," the fiction that *he* accepts as fiction because it "results from feeling." Moving momentarily into his former "we" stance (stanza 6), the speaker affirms the place of thought as abstraction in his experience and in his various expressions of experience (getting it straight at the Sorbonne). But his dominant stance here at the end of the canto and the poem as a whole is his new "I" stance and its affirmation of thought informed ("flicked") by feeling. He embraces the simple pleasure of belief free for the moment from doubt, the personal and newly intense sense of reality that he can *name,* however fleetingly.

The dual function or role of the aphorisms in this and all of Stevens's meditative verse is the result of a lifelong interest in the technique of aphoristic expression. As initiating statements producing an authoritative effect, aphorisms give the reader a sense that the poetic experience begins with thought and retains an anchor in it. As parts of a compendium, taken in context with their respective cantos and in interaction with each other, aphorisms also provide a simulacrum of the process of moving from thought to feeling—from abstraction to pleasure.

Understanding aphorism as the basic unit of Stevens's expression in these later poems and in the "amassing harmony" of his works as a whole brings to mind again that early journal entry:

> There are no end of gnomes that might influence people—but do not. When you first feel the truth of, say, an epigram, you feel like making it a rule of conduct. But this one is displaced by that, and things go on in their accustomed way.

8. Autograph jottings (two aphoristic entries and then a list of readings).

The best prose story will be that which presents ordinary life most faithfully; the best poetry will be rhetorical criticism.

The indefinable personal note which is everything in literature

Barthé Saints Rest
St. Augustine's Confessions
Bunyan's Grace Abounding.
South's Sermons,
The constant reflection on nature is freed, like the constant thought about art,
Sir Henry Taylor's Autobiography
Amiel's Journal
Mrs Carlyle
Boswell & Vicar of Wakefield
Newton's Life & Himself

Such an observation sums up the use of aphorism in Stevens's poetry. He began with a love for the "feel of truth" in aphorism despite his belief that such truth is tentative. Throughout the series of experiments that constituted his poetic career he retained a belief in the understanding that aphorism gives the mind and in the resulting self-discovery that it enables the mind to make and to which it gives expression. And always he found consolation and invigoration in the power of aphorism as a form of human expression which enables man to capture experience, however minute that experience might be, however temporary his hold upon it.

Appendix A

Miles's Argument for the Three Sentence Types in English

This appendix briefly summarizes Miles's discussion of the three sentence types in English.[1] Miles's adjectival sentence is characterized by "the infrequent verb, heavily loaded with noun modifications," as in the following passage from Huxley's "Uniqueness of Man *(Man in the Modern World):*

> Man's opinion of his own position in relation to the rest of the animals has swung pendulum-wise between too great or too little a conceit of himself, fixing now too large a gap between himself and the animals, now too small. The gap, of course, can be diminished or increased at either the animal or the human end. One can, like Descartes, make animals too mechanical, or, like most unsophisticated people, humanize them too much. Or one can work at the human end of the gap, and then either dehumanize one's own kind into an animal species like any other, or superhumanize it into being a little lower than the angels.

Miles says of this passage that "the many epithets—*too great, too little, too small, animal, human mechanical*—are crucial to the thought and overweigh the fewer verbs, themselves nearly adjectival—*has swung, can be diminished, can work, dehumanize, superhumanize.* Such proportioning is accentuated by a choice of participial modifiers like *fixing* instead of verb clauses with *which.*" Miles notes that in general such an adjectival style "changes the natural order of materials in order to effect control over them before predication.... As strong assumptions are made, subjects are tremendously amplified without the activity of predication, because inherent qualities rather than new relations are stressed. Sentences are lengthy, rounded, suspended, with a great deal of elaborately connected material. Words can be unusual, coined, figured; sounds can be mouth-filling, even harsh; and meanings can be implied, oblique, symbolic" (Miles, 8).

A second sentence type, the connective-subordinative, is characterized by its expression of complex relationships between ideas through the use of connectives and subordination. One of Miles's examples is from Bertrand Russell's essay, "Philosophy's Ulterior Motives":

Philosophy, as opposed to science, springs from a kind of self-assertion: a belief that our purposes have an important relation to the purposes of the universe, and that, in the long run, the course of events is bound to be, on the whole, such as we should wish. Science abandoned this kind of optimism, but is being led towards another: that we, by our intelligence, can make the world such as to satisfy a large proportion of our desires: This is a practical, as opposed to a metaphysical, optimism. I hope it will not seem to future generations as foolish as that of Dr. Pangloss.

Here the sentences tend to contain a balance between the number of adjectives and verbs used and between the number of independent and dependent clauses. Connected words—"as opposed to," "from . . . to," "belief that," "and that," "but," "such as"—determine the relationship between substantives and introduce clauses in subordinate relation to independent clauses. Thus, they tend to carry the thought of the passage. Miles's general conclusion about the style resulting from the use primarily of this type of sentence is that it is "classical inasmuch as logic, subordination, and poise are its strong characteristics." Writers utilizing the connective-subordinative sentence "share with Russell his moderate alternatives . . . his strong substantial sense of nouns, phrases and relative clauses" which reflect "in their close design a weighing and arguing, and active and balancing mind and mode of thought . . . ." (Miles, 6-7).

Among other passages from Emerson, Miles uses the following one from "Self-Reliance" in her efforts to define her third, aphoristic, sentence type:

Trust thyself: every heart vibrates to that iron string. Accept the place the divine Providence has found for you; the society of your contemporaries, the connexion of events. Great men have always done so, and confided themselves childlike to the genius of their age, betraying their perception that the Eternal was stirring at their heart, working through their hands, predominating in all their being. And we are now men, and must accept in the highest mind the same transcendent destiny; and not pinched in a corner, not cowards fleeing before a revolution, but redeemers and benefactors, pious aspirants to be noble clay plastic under the Almighty effort, let us advance and advance on Chaos and the Dark.

Here the emphases on the verb and the accompanying lack of modifiers, subordinative clauses, and connectives produces a style that is curt and pointed in its refusal to qualify terms, give importance to certain ideas through the subordination of others, or make explicit the relationship of ideas between one sentence and another. In noting that Emerson's critics have complained that his sentences seem "to repel rather than to attract each other," Miles observes that "the absence of strong explicit connectives does not mean the absence of strong implied connections. . . . The argument moves between particular and general, and from key word to key word." Miles demonstrates the subtleties of her argument in the following passage:

Such thought is logical, even syllogistic. The general: All men are mortal; the particular: Socrates is a man; the conclusion: Therefore Socrates is mortal. You and I participate in this truth. But the *and's* and *therefore's* have been omitted or have been used with relative infrequency. In other words, the logical relation of all to one is present, but not the explicit links in the steps of relation. Further, Emerson might begin with what we would call an untenable premise: All men are immortal. He would feel this intuitively—"The blazing of evidence of immortality," the "gleam of light which flashes across his mind from within"— and so he would base upon it his logical argument for anyone and for us. And further, he would treat key words like *man* in a special way, including in them all their degrees of evaluative reference from lowest to highest; so that "man" would mean man in his limitless degree of spirit, as well as in his limiting degree of body, thus supporting by definition, implicit or explicit, the relation between *man* and *immortal* that the syllogism makes. It is as if Emerson were essentially satisfied to say: All men are men (with all men's limitations and potentialities); a man acts like a man. The connective *therefore's* and adjectival *mortal's* are minimal; the subject-predicate *Men are, a man is,* central. (Miles, 70-71)

Appendix B

Two Further Examples of Aphorisms Used as Epigraphs

Canto xxiv from "An Ordinary Evening in New Haven":

Frank Doggett notes that in Boethius's *De Consolatione Philosophiae* (The Consolations of Philosophy) there is an elaborate set of personifications or names that Boethius gives to the various forms taken by philosophy's power of consolation.[1] For Stevens, by contrast, "The consolations of space are *nameless things;*" and the rest of the poem explains what he means by this statement. "Space" seems to be a synecdoche for nature. The consolations that nature offers are not those of static belief or attitude which can be expressed in names, but rather, those of change, and therefore of variety. Winter, the time of stasis in belief or attitude, is characterized as a time of "neurosis." Summer is a time of "genius," the zenith of vitality and creativity, and the antithesis of "neurosis." In summer, the pressure of such dynamism explodes static beliefs ("the *statue* of Jove") and not only opens the way to new and more viable ones but provides the impetus to partly find, partly make such new combinations of "self" and not self ("space"). These, too, will—in time—necessarily crystallize into neurotically static beliefs, just as summer inevitably moves into winter. But in the poem the appearance of the statue is nowhere in sight as the narrator takes pleasure in the fresh sense of life which succeeds both the explosion of an old belief and the chaos which follows it and accompanies the first awareness that a new belief (a new "yes") exists, however amorphous. Stevens's own belief is not in any particular view of reality, but in reality's potential for an unlimited multiplicity of interpretations by the self and therefore for unlimited possibilities of change and variety in the self—though in any particular time or place both kinds of possibilities would be limited.

This canto of the poem thus begins with an abstraction and ends with a vivid characterization of the state of feeling which precedes the state of mind in which abstraction becomes possible.

"Reality Is the Activity of the Most August Imagination":

In this poem-title epigraph, Stevens is echoing his own *Adagia* entries ("The great conquest is the conquest of reality," *OP,* 168). Reality in this poem is presented metaphorically as a night lit by the moon and stars; but not, as Ronald Sukenick explains, "one of a traditional or outworn artifice such as might be seen in Vienna or Venice—it is not a traditional reality that has come to an end, static, like a artifact from a glasswork."[2] For the speaker reality must be seen as flux itself, presented in the last five stanzas of the poem as the activity of the imagination. That activity is equaled with the mind's perception not of moonlight itself but of its illumination of objects and transformations of them—transformations particularized in the body of the poem by words emphasizing "activity"—"crush," "grinding," "vigor," "glittering," "emerged," "moved," "dissolved," "change," "transformations," "*approaching* form," "*suddenly* denying itself away," "insolid *billowing* of the solid." What is important for the purposes of this study is the way the poem is prefaced by an abstract statement in the title-aphorism defining the nature of reality and then moves in the poem itself to the concreteness of a narrative ("Last Friday... We drove from Cornwall to Hartford, late") which, with its accompanying (and equally important) images, particularizes the title-statement.

Notes

Chapter 1

1. A.R. Ammons, *Sphere: The Form of Motion* (New York: Norton, 1974), p. 17. All italics throughout are those of the present author unless otherwise indicated.

2. *View* (September, 1940 and October, 1942).

3. See also B. Coyle, "An Anchorage of Thought: The Study of Aphorism in Wallace Stevens's Poetry," *PMLA* 91 (1976), pp. 206-222.

4. See Frank Doggett, "Abstraction and Wallace Stevens," *Criticism* 2 (1960), pp. 23-37; *Stevens' Poetry of Thought* (Baltimore: John Hopkins Press, 1966); idem, "Stevens' Later Poetry," *Critics on Wallace Stevens,* ed. Peter L. McNamara (Coral Gables, Florida: University of Miami, 1972), pp. 113-126; A. Walton Litz, *Introspective Voyager: The Poetic Development of Wallace Stevens* (New York: Oxford University Press, 1972); Helen Vendler, *On Extended Wings: Wallace Stevens' Longer Poems* (Cambridge, Mass.: Harvard University Press, 1969).

5. Daniel Tomkins, "'To Abstract Reality': Abstract Language and the Intrusion of Consciousness in Wallace Stevens," *American Literature* XLV: 1, pp. 88-89.

6. *The Rock,* the last grouping of poems in *The Collected Poems,* was never published as a volume.

7. Frank Doggett, "Stevens' Later Poetry," p. 119.

8. Ibid.

9. Barbara Herrnstein Smith, *Poetic Closure* (Chicago: University of Chicago Press, 1968). "Finality" is described by Smith as a reader's sense that a "terminal point in a sequence" has been reached; "stability," as the "sense of ultimate composure" the reader feels when, at the end of a sequence, he has "no further expectation." (pp. 35-36, 45).

10. Ibid., p. 6.

11. Wallace Stevens, *Opus Posthumous,* ed. Samuel French Morse (New York: Alfred A. Knopf, 1957), p. 157. Hereafter references will be cited in text.

12. Smith, *Poetic Closure,* p. 163.

13. Wallace Stevens, *The Collected Poems of Wallace Stevens* (New York: Alfred A. Knopf, 1954), p. 145. Hereafter references will be cited in text.

14. Smith, *Poetic Closure,* p. 164.

15. Ibid., pp. 11-13.

16. Smith explores all these boundary effects in her study of closure.

17. Smith, *Poetic Closure*, p. 6.

18. Frank Doggett, "Stevens' Later Poetry," p. 119.

19. Josephine Miles, *Style and Proportion: The Language of Prose and Poetry* (Boston: Little Brown, 1967).

20. For a fuller explanation of Miles's three sentence types see Appendix A.

21. Smith, *Poetic Closure*, p. 182.

22. Ibid.

23. Ibid., p. 183.

24. W.H. Auden, *The Viking Book of Aphorism* (New York: Viking Press, 1966), p. ii.

25. See Smith's extensive analysis of Lessing's terms, *Erwartung* and *Aufschluss* in her study of "Epigram and Epigrammatic," in *Poetic Closure*, chapter 5. "Predetermination" is Smith's term, which she discusses generally on pp. 154-57.

26. A. Walton Litz, *Introspective Voyager*, p. 233.

27. Francis Bacon, *Works,* eds. Spedding, Ellis and Heath, vol. 5 (London, 1861), p. 89.

28. Ibid., p. 89.

29. Ronald Sukenick, *Wallace Stevens: Musing the Obscure* (New York: New York University Press, 1967), pp. 10-11.

30. Wallace Stevens, *Letters of Wallace Stevens,* ed. Holly Stevens (New York: Alfred A. Knopf, 1954), p. 91. Hereafter references will be cited in text.

31. I cannot do justice here to the subtleties of Frank Doggett's analysis of this same poem in relation to William James's idea of pluralism. While Doggett calls the aphorisms "the abstract element" in the poem and does not offer them as Stevens's ultimate truths, he ignores the pastness in the poem and takes the aphorisms as givens on the nongivenness of reality: "Pluralism is an intuition of reality in Stevens'["On the Road Home"]. The abstract element becomes the poet's means of certain realizations.... silence for Stevens has implications of non-being and of a universe indifferent to man.... And in contrast with that silence he enters intensely his own immediate sense of the round night and the warm fragrant autumn. The idea has transformed his experience." ("Abstraction and Wallace Stevens," p. 32). But another way to understand *the* silence, so parallel in its singularity to *the* truth that the speakers denied, is that it enters in the last stanza as if in comic answer to their denials which have begun to go flat. The silence puts an end to what the givens claim and initiates the possibility of a truth.

32. *Selected Longer Poems* (New York: Norton, 1972), p. 43.

Chapter 2

1. See Samuel French Morse's introduction to Wallace Stevens, *Opus Posthumous* (New York: Alfred A. Knopf, 1957—Hereafter references will be cited in text.) p. xxxi, and A. Walton Litz, "Particles of Order, The Unpublished *Adagia,*" in *Wallace Stevens: A Celebration,* eds. Frank Doggett and Robert Buttel (New Jersey: Princeton University Press, 1980), pp. 57-58.

2. My translation of the French: "the destination of man is to increase in the feeling of joy, to grow in unlimited energy, and to fight with all that he is the principle of debasement and sadness."

3. Perhaps this last example is the first formulation of the aphorism discussed above, p. 4: "Lean encyclopaedists inscribe an Iliad/There's a weltanschauung of the penny pad." Holly Stevens's "Letter excerpts" given above are from *Letters of Wallace Stevens*, pp. 79, 80, 108, and 87 respectively.

4. The *Adagia* has been treated by some Stevens's critics as a storehouse of didactic comments, any one of which can be used to make the poet say with great finality what one wants to hear. A critic concerned, for example, with Stevens's "bad habit of philosophizing" will find convenient corroboration in "The momentum of the mind is all toward abstraction" or "The poem in which the poet has chosen for his subject a philosophical theme should result in the poem of poems." but as shall be discussed the *Adagia* has a context. An individual entry which so nearly expresses the particular point a critic wants to make is surrounded by hundreds of other equally compelling ones which may or may not reinforce the one selected. In the sum of the parts there are not merely the parts, though Stevens himself can be quoted as claiming the opposite.

5. *Opus Posthumous*, pp. 162, 158, 170, 175, 173.

6. A Walton Litz, *Introspective Voyager*, p. 10.

7. See Litz's Appendix B, pp. 302-16, for a reprinting of all the suites to be discussed in this chapter—"Carnet du Voyage," "Phases," and "Lettres d'un Soldat." Litz gives cogent arguments for the version of each suite he thinks closest to a final version, and provides extensive notes on the circumstances surrounding Stevens's choice and arrangement of the poem-parts in each suite.

8. "Justice without force is a contradiction because there will always be the unjust; but force without justice is a reprehension."

9. For different emphasis, Litz offers explanations of these four titles of poem groups. (See *Introspective Voyager*, pp. 62, 91, 97, 106.) Particularly interesting in light of the present analysis of the aphoristic quality of the early poem-suites in general is Litz's observation about the "self-deprecating title 'Pecksniffiana'.... Readers of Dickens... will remember the pompous and oracular Mr. Pecksniff, Architect,... whose pupils were asked to draw cathedrals *from every possible angle....*"

10. In addition to the Lermercier aphorisms introducing each of Stevens's poems, there is a French epigraph as well which Stevens took from André Chevrillon's preface to the young soldiers posthumous letters: "Combattre avec ses frères, à sa place, à son rang, avec des yeux dessillés, sans espoir de gloire et de profit, et simplement parce que telle est la loi, voilà le commandement que donne le dieu au guerrier Arjuna, quand celui-ci doute s'il doit se détourner de l'absolu pour le cauchemar humain de la bataille.... Simplement, du'Arjuna bande son arc avec les autres Kshettryas!" (Litz translates: To fight with his brothers, at his own place, in his own rank, with open eyes, without hope of glory or of gain, and simply because such is the law: This is the commandment of the god to the warrior Arjuna, who had doubted whether he were right in turning from the absolute to take part in the human nightmare of war.... Plainly, it is for Arjuna to bend his bow among the other Kshettryas!)
    The acceptance of war suggested here is important to the development of the suite. The fact that the epigraph does this in French may also be significant for the use of the French aphorisms throughout the suite: as the final poem in the suite mitigates the bitterness of Stevens's English poems, so this epigraph mitigates, in their own language, the idealism of

Lemercier's French aphorisms. To assure this purpose Stevens sent special instructions to his editor that any English translations of the aphorisms were to be placed in an appendix and not with the text itself (*L,* 202).

11. "Never has the majesty of the night afforded me such consolation as in these accumulations of trials. Venus, sparkling, is my love." (Translations are those of the present author unless otherwise indicated.)

12. The allusion to Venus comes in the last stanza of the poem. During some times of the year, Venus, not part of a constellation, can still be seen in the west after the sun has risen and other stars have vanished; hence the image of her constancy—"She will leap back from the swift constellations,/ As they enter the place of their western/Seclusion."

13. "My dearly beloved Mother.... Because of that which comes from your heart, I have such confidence in your courage that at the present hour this certitude is my greatest comfort. I know that my mother possesses that freedom of love that permits her to contemplate the universal spectacle."

14. "If you could see the security of the small forest animals, the grey field mice! The other day, in our encampment, I watched the movement of these creatures. They were as pretty as a Japanese painting, with the insides of their ears rosy as a shell."

15. "What is necessary is that we recognize that love and beauty triumph in all violence."

16. Frank Doggett, "Stevens' Later Poetry," p. 119.

Chapter 3

1. The separate sections of his long meditative poems operate somewhat like poem-parts, suggesting a way in which the early poem-suites and poem groups are experiments which prefigure the later, canto poems.

2. See Robert Buttel's *Wallace Stevens: The Making of Harmonium* (New Jersey: Princeton University Press, 1967), pp. 188-90 for the entire letter from Williams.

3. A. Walton Litz, *Introspective Voyager,* p. 38.

4. See Stevens's essay, "The Noble Rider and The Sound of Words," reprinted in *The Necessary Angel* (New York: Vintage, 1951), pp. 3-36.

5. See William Pratt, *The Imagist Poem* (New York: Dutton, 1963), p. 29.

6. Vendler cites the *Letters,* p. 240, for Stevens's later "intellectual remarks to Henry Church: 'that the last section was intended to convey despair,' that section xii existed to convey 'the compulsion frequently back of the things that we do'...." See *On Extended Wings,* p. 76.

7. These phrases are those of the present author but are based on a reading of Stanley K. Coffman, *Imagism: A Chapter for the History of Modern Poetry,* (Norman, Oklahoma: University of Oklahoma Press, 1951) and Pratt, *The Imagist Poem.*

8. Vendler uses the word "tautalogical" when discussing parts of this poem. See *On Extended Wings,* p. 78.

9. Barbara Smith, *Poetic Closure* (Chicago: University of Chicago Press, 1968), p. 207.

10. Cf. "Variations on a Summer Day" and "Six Significant Landscapes."

11. "Debris of Life and Mind," "Pieces," and "Extracts from the Academy of Fine Ideas," for example.

12. Stevens wrote to William Rose Benet, who wished to include some of Stevens's poems in an anthology, "I think I should select from poems as my favorite the Emperor of Ice Cream" (*L*, 263).

13. Samuel French Morse says this of "The Snow Man" in his introduction to Wallace Stevens, *Opus Posthumous*, p. xxxiv.

14. Frank Doggett, *Stevens' Poetry of Thought*, p. 130.

15. In addition to the bracketed numbers, two words of my own have been placed in brackets to indicate a turn of thought implied by the speaker.

16. See Appendix A for a discussion of Josephine Miles's account of the argumentativeness of subordinate and coordinate conjunctions.

17. "Squamous," according to Sukenick, means "covered with scales, sometimes with reference to a kind of armor and, also, part of the bone structure of the temple" (See Ronald Sukenick, *Wallace Stevens: Musing the Obscure*, p. 104). I am indebted to Sukenick for his close reading of the poem which assisted me in my analysis of the relationship between the opening and closing propositions and the body of the poem.

Chapter 4

1. Frank Doggett, "Stevens' Later Poetry," p. 119.

2. Joseph N. Riddel, *The Clairvoyant Eye: The Poetry and Poetics of Wallace Stevens* (Baton Rouge, Louisiana: Louisiana State University Press, 1967), p. 73.

3. The idea would be paraphrased as follows: Looking at beliefs as "fictive things" (as various but always only ideas of ordering reality) makes the didactic mind uncomfortable ("Makes widows wince"). But such ideas "wink as they will" (tend to come to us, to gleam or flash intuitively, rapidly, unpredictably, as if beyond our will to control their coming to us). In fact, they "wink most" (come to us most quickly, most mischievously, and most fortunately) when we are confronted with "widows" (a metaphor for man's latent desire to have an impenetrable, fixed view of reality).

4. An "epigraph," in the strict sense, is an apposite quotation such as Stevens took from the Lemercier letters to introduce each of its poem-parts in "Lettres d'un Soldat." The term will be used here to apply to those aphorisms which either stand physically apart from a poetic text or appear in the first line and stand syntactically apart from the action of the poem as a self-contained statement. In both cases, the term will apply to those poems which begin with a aphoristic statement of the poem's significance which is so separate from the poem's narrative that it functions like an epigraph.

5. "Lunar Paraphrase" and "Death of a Soldier" were the only poems Stevens republished from the poem-suite, *Lettres d'un Soldat*; both poems contain their own epigraphic units and are not dependent upon those provided by the French epigraphs. Shown in these pages is Stevens's autograph copy of "Lunar Paraphrase" in which the French has been rather dramatically struck out.

6. An analysis of Canto XXIV from "An Ordinary Evening" and the poem "Reality Is an Activity of the Most August Imagination" is not essential to my point in merely citing these poems as examples of Stevens's use of epigraphlike aphorisms. I have placed my analysis of each poem in Appendix B.

7. I take "brune" to be a short form of "brunet" meaning dark or brown.

8. Or, in the case of the epigraphlike aphorism in the two examples cited earlier, what "reality *is*" or what the "consolations of space *are.*"

9. These last two stanzas of the poem—with their use of celebrative infinitives, their lack of rhyme or strict meter, and their image of the boat rushing brightly through the summer air— are in sharp contrast to the first four stanzas of the poem where self-pitying speaker ("a most inappropriate man/In a most unpropitious place") laments the fact that he cannot free himself of the stale romantic. Dominating these earlier stanzas are images of a boat caught in a whirlpool and the accompanying predominance of ironic techniques—jingling rhymes, anapests, and a variety of repetitive devices such as frequent anaphora, abundant alliteration, assonance, and other sound echoes like "inappropriate... unpropitious," "mustiest... vertiginous... vapidest." Terrence Joseph King points out these techniques of the first four stanzas in "An Effect of Ease: Stanzaic Structure in the Early Poetry of Wallace Stevens" (Ph.D. dissertation, University of Michigan, 1970), p. 21.

10. Ronald Sukenick, *Musing the Obscure,* p. 54.

11. Or, as Stevens says of *Three Travelers Watch a Sunrise,* "the play is simply intended to demonstrate that just as objects in nature offset us, as for example, 'Dead trees do not resemble/Beaten drums,' so, on the other hand, we affect objects in nature by projecting our moods, emotions etc: 'an old man from Pekin/Observes sunrise,/Through Pekin, reddening.'" (*L,* 195)

12. Northrop Frye, "The Realistic Oriole: A Study of Wallace Stevens," *Hudson Review* X (Autumn 1957), p. 103.

13. Stevens once told R.L. Latimer (in an assertion that his titles are always important to the meaning of his poems): "Very often the title occurs to me before anything else occurs to me" (*L,* 297).

14. Actually the unit I'm calling the "epigraph" in II closes that canto and functions as part of the epigraph to III. There is an implied "since" between the two units which make them act as one, thus both closing II and introducing III in one movement.

15. This last canto goes on to give examples of how plainness is the effect or cause of savagery. But note how it ends with a third example of how spring and autumn are the plain effects of a savage or violent change, which, once it has occurred, has a soothing effect, as of a desire satisfied. This ending to canto IV ties together the conflicting perspectives in the aphorisms from the preceding three cantos—the uniqueness of the plain version, its inseparability from desire (or imagination), its being an effect of violent change.

16. See "Like Decorations in a Nigger Cemetery," and "Variations on a Summer Day."

Appendix A

1. Josephine Miles, *Style and Proportion: The Language of Prose and Poetry* (Boston: Little Brown, 1967), chapter 1. Specific page references will be given in text.

Appendix B

1. Frank Doggett, "Stevens' Later Poetry," p. 117.

2. Ronald Sukenick, *Musing the Obscure,* p. 199.

Bibliography

Ammons, A.R. *Sphere: The Form of Motion*. New York: Norton, 1974.

Auden, W.H. *The Viking Book of Aphorism*. New York: Viking Press, 1966.

Bacon, Francis. *Works*. vol. V. Edited by Spedding, Ellis, and Heath. London: ,1861.

Buttel, Robert. *Wallace Stevens: The Making of Harmonium*. Princeton, New Jersey: Princeton University Press, 1967.

Coffman, Stanley K. *Imagism: A Chapter for the History of Modern Poetry*. Norman, Oklahoma, University of Oklahoma Press, 1951.

Coyle, Beverly, "An Anchorage of Thought: The Study of Aphorism in Wallace Stevens's Poetry." *PMLA* 91 (1976): 206-22.

Doggett, Frank. "Abstraction and Wallace Stevens." *Criticism* 2 (1960): 23-37.

_____. *Stevens' Poetry of Thought*. Baltimore: Johns Hopkins Press, 1966.

_____. "Stevens' Later Poetry.' In *Critics on Wallace Stevens*, ed. Peter L. McNamara, pp. 113-126. Coral Gables, Florida: University of Miami, 1972.

Frye, Northrup. "The Realistic Oriole: A Study of Wallace Stevens." *Hudson Review* X (Autumn 1957): 353-70.

King, Terrence Joseph. "An Effect of Ease: Stanzaic Structure in the Early Poetry of Wallace Stevens." Ph.D. dissertation, University of Michigan, 1970.

Litz, A. Walton. *Introspective Voyager: The Poetic Development of Wallace Stevens*. New York: Oxford University Press, 1972.

_____. "Particles of Order, the Unpublished *Adagia*." In *Wallace Stevens: A Celebration*, eds. Frank Doggett and Robert Buttel, pp. 57-77. Princeton, New Jersey: Princeton University Press, 1980.

Miles, Josephine. *Style and Proportion: The Language of Prose and Poetry*. Boston: Little Brown, 1967.

Pratt, William. *The Imagist Poem*. New York: Dutton, 1963.

Riddel, Joseph N. *The Clairvoyant Eye: The Poetry and Poetics of Wallace Stevens*. Baton Rouge, Louisiana: Louisiana State University Press, 1965.

Smith, Barbara Herrnstein. *Poetic Closure*. Chicago: The University of Chicago Press, 1968.

Stevens, Wallace. *The Collected Poems of Wallace Stevens*. New York: Alfred A. Knopf, 1954.

_____. *Letters of Wallace Stevens*. Ed. Holly Stevens. New York: Alfred A. Knopf, 1954.

_____. *The Necessary Angel*. New York: Vintage, 1951.

_____. *Opus Posthumous*. Ed. Samuel French Morse. New York: Alfred A. Knopf, 1957.

Sukenick, Ronald. *Wallace Stevens: Musing the Obscure*. New York: New York Unversity Press, 1967.

Tomkins, Daniel. "'To Abstract Reality': Abstract Language and the Intrusion of Consciousness in Wallace Stevens." *American Literature* XLV: 1: 88-97.

Vendler, Helen Hennessy. *On Extended Wings: Wallace Stevens' Longer Poems.* Cambridge, Mass.: Harvard University Press, 1969.

Winters, Yvor. *In Defense of Reason.* Denver, Colorado: University of Denver Press, 1947.

Index